Mina's Revolution

Mehrnoosh Mazarei

Library of Congress Control Number: <u>2015914756</u>
CreateSpace Independent Publishing Platform,
North Charleston, SC
ISBN: 1517017157
ISBN-13 9781517017156

Cover design and cover artwork by Mokhtar Paki of
<u>www.mokhtarimage.com</u>

*To the free-spirited women of both my
countries, Iran and America*

Acknowledgments

I am thankful to Tom Jenks, Raha Namy, Stephanie Reents and Diane Grant for helping in the process of editing of this book.

I would like to express my gratitude to all those who provided support by reading, commenting, and assisting in the proofreading and design of this book, including but not limited to Fariba Rofougaran, Malihe Tirehgl, Bijan Bijari, Sara Amir, Jinus Saleh, Azarnoush Mazarei, Mehrdad Asaadi and Zohreh Ghahramani.

Above all I want to thank my husband, Khosrow Davami, and my daughter Asal Sepassi who supported and encouraged me throughout writing this book.

The historian will tell you what happened.
The novelist will tell you what it felt like.
E. L. Doctorow

Contents

Los Angeles - Sept. 10th 2001

<u>11 a.m.</u>

The airline associates were about to close the gate when Mina arrived. A major accident on the 405 freeway had delayed her. One of the crew members looked at her boarding pass and politely said, "Welcome Ms. Shabani. I'm glad you were able to make it."

As Mina got comfortable in her seat, the flight attendant came over and asked for her drink choice.
"Gin and tonic please."

The man sitting next to Mina set aside his newspaper and ordered a Chivas on the rocks.

After finishing her drink, Mina took out her laptop from the leather briefcase she had stored under her seat, plugged it into the outlet in front of her, and established connection to her Internet service provider. Her eyes scanned the long list of her email in inbox. Nothing new from her daughter Shirin. She opened an email from her boss and read his last recommendations for the meeting she was going to attend the next day in New York.

It was eight years since Mina had seen Shirin. In all those years, she had not received a response to any of her calls, letters, or emails - except for the one she had sent out a week ago.

She found the email in the archive and opened it. Short and cold:

In your last email you mentioned your trip to New York on Sept. 11. I can meet you that day, but probably not for dinner as you asked. Call me when you get here.

Shirin Pashaee

"What would you like to have for lunch, Ms. Shabani?" It was the flight attendant again.

Mina closed the laptop, picked up the lunch menu, and asked for the chicken breast with sautéed vegetables and a glass of chilled Chardonnay. "Can I also have a New York Times?"

"Are you going back home?" Mina turned toward the voice. It was the man in the aisle seat - an attractive man with short salt-and-pepper hair, in a gray suit and loose tie.

"Oh no, just a short trip to New York."

"You're dressed like a New Yorker." His affectionate eyes fixed on Mina's for a second. Then, he lowered his eyes and added, "Your outfit is lovely."

"Oh, thanks." Mina had on a beige V-neck silk top, a brown, knee-length skirt, and two small dangling earrings plated with the Nishabour turquoise that

Mother had sent her from Iran years ago. Her mid-length straight brown hair with reddish, highlighted streaks was styled by Farideh, her hairdresser in Westwood, or as Farideh always preferred to say, in Tehrangeles.

"You have an interesting accent," he said.

"I'm originally from Iran, but I consider myself more of an American these days," Mina replied.

"Awesome! You are Persian."

I could also be a Turk, Kurd, Lur, Turkmen, Baluchi, Armenian or Arab, Mina thought, but she answered, "Yes, I am a Persian Iranian."

"I can say couple of Arabic words," the man said and continued in a funny accent. "Alsalaamu Alykum."

Mina concealed her smile and said, "Great! I know some Arabic words too, but we don't use this phrase for greeting people as Arabs do. We simply say "Salaam" in Farsi, which is our official language in ee-raan." She emphasized on the pronunciation of ee-raan.

She was not irritated or offended by this conversation the way she was when she first came to America, especially when people asked if they rode on camels in Eye-ran. Father always boasted about Persians being Aryans as a superior race. He even admired Reza shah, the Shah's father, for allying with Hitler and Germans during World War II. He said, "We are connected with Germans, they are Aryans!" He resented the British and Allies for coming to Iran after the war and sending Reza Shah into exile and bringing the Shah, a young man in his twenties, to power He began to hate the Americans and the CIA even more when they arranged a massive coup d'état against

Mosaddegh, his beloved prime minister, and brought the Shah back after he had fled Iran. The coup d'etat coincided with Father's first trip to Tehran, back when he was in his twenties. Mina had been born a year before. Father talked about his memory of that day over and over. At one point, he had been trapped between the CIA-backed mobs who striped Mosaddegh of power and Mosaddegh's supporters. Either side could have killed him. After that day, Father linked any political wrongdoing in the world, even the assassination of President Kennedy, to the CIA.

The flight attendant brought their lunch. Without turning the laptop off, Mina placed it on the compartment between the two seats and started eating.

"How long have you been in this country?" the man asked.

"More than twenty years," Mina replied.

"Did you leave before the Revolution?"

"No, just shortly after."

"You must be very clever to have escaped all those fundamental religious restrictions."

Mina's hand involuntarily rose to her forehead. With the tip of her middle finger, she stroked the remainder of a wound, which could hardly be seen now.

"It was definitely not easy," she murmured, then turned her face away and continued eating her lunch. No, not easy at all. It was even harder after she escaped them.

Everything in the dessert menu seemed delicious. Mina usually did not have a problem choosing a main course, but it was hard to choose a dessert; she loved them all. The tiramisu looked the best. Still, she liked the raspberry chocolate cake, the creme brûlée, the fresh fruit dish, and the pecan caramel cheesecake. While she was studying the other items on the menu, a beep from her computer informed her of a new email.

"The raspberry chocolate cake and one shot of espresso. Please add a piece of lemon peel on the side," said Mina, as she handed the dessert menu back to flight attendant and picked up the laptop.

"Maman, I can only meet you over breakfast tomorrow morning. I am busy the rest of the day. Let's meet at 8:30 at the place you suggested, the *Windows of the World* at the World Trade Center. I can walk to my office after the breakfast."

After Mina finished the dessert, ready for some rest, she took out a book from her briefcase. The flight attendant helped her adjust her seat, then withdrew a pillow and blanket from the compartment and handed them to her. After all these first class flights in the past several years, Mina still got a kick of being pampered by the crew members.

She opened the book and found the page that she had read last. Not even one third. Being an avid reader, she should have been done with it by now. It was an English translation of Anna Karenina. She had read the Farsi version years ago when she was only sixteen. She started to read but could not concentrate. Shirin had called her "Maman" again! Could they get along again? They did not know each other well even when they lived together. What were her social and political interests? Did she have a boyfriend? Would she consider coming back to LA? Would she be interested to know Mina better?

Shirin barely knew about the conditions under which Mina and Hamid, had grown up. They never talked about Iran, and surely Hamid hadn't told Shirin about his childhood. He had tried hard to wipe out all the bad memories; he probably does not even remember them himself.

Mina laid the book on her lap and closed her eyes.

• • •

Nov. 13, 1979 / New York

The Imperial Majesty of Iran, the foil-stamped inscription on the passport, caught the officer's eye. She opened the passport, started thumbing through it, and stopped at the Islamic Republic of Iran's exit stamp. She flipped back to the passport's photo, paused a moment, then lifted her head and looked suspiciously at Mina. "Is this you?"

Mina nodded, her heart beginning to beat faster. The photo was from a couple of years earlier, when she had first planned on coming to America. Her hair had been long and straight and she had worn a lot of makeup. She touched her hair with the palm of her right hand. With short curly hair and no makeup, Mina looked different now. She also weighed more. Her waist was wider and her breasts were swollen. She touched her belly gently.

The officer examined the American visa stamped on the middle page of passport. The visa was valid for another full year. The burgundy-colored cover looked lighter in the officer's dark-skinned hand. The officer closed the passport, wrote a note on a form, and handed both to Mina. "Take this form with you to the immigration office," she pointed to a glass door and a long line of people waiting for approval to enter USA.

"Vaat?" Mina said, "Sorry, I do not under estand."

The officer got up and led Mina over to the immigration office. Handing the form and Mina's passport to one of the men sitting behind a desk, the officer exchanged some words with him then went back to her station without even glancing at Mina. Now that Mina could see "Immigration Office" written on the glass door, she understood what the officer had meant. She was embarrassed.

The office was small with three desks, six chairs, and a few photos on the wall.

A young officer with a pale mustache looked at Mina's documents and asked for her ticket. He then gave the ticket to another officer and talked to him briefly. The second man left the office with Mina's ticket. Mina panicked. What is he doing? Should she follow him? She looked at the first officer. He was not paying attention to her. If he wanted her to go with him, shouldn't he say so? Or at least signal her? Maybe she was missing something. She opened her mouth to ask the officer, but decided to keep silence. She would wait. If they wanted her to do anything, they would tell her. Should she sit?

Mina busied herself with the pictures. Three frames hung on the wall, each almost 50 by 40 centimeters. Three men in ties and suits. Among them, Mina only recognized President Jimmy Carter; his light hair and light eyes were similar to President Kennedy's.

The officer eventually came back, carrying Mina's two suitcases. He put them down in front of her and with

7

a hand gesture, asked Mina to unlock them.

"You have so many books!" he exclaimed. "Why are you bringing them to the U.S.?"

"Maybe she is here to make us believe we are the big Satan!" the other officer mocked.

Both officers snickered, and each took a book from the suitcase and leafed through it. One of the officers stopped at a picture. "Is this Komeini's son?" he asked.

Mina could not restrain a sarcastic smile. The picture was one of the leftist rebels killed in a fight with the Shah's secret agents, the SAVAK. Mina's grin added to the men's suspicion. "Oh... you think it is funny! I wonder if you were as amused when you took our boys hostage."

Without understanding the man, Mina heard his anger.

"What do you think about Komeini?" the other officer asked.

Mina smiled naively and did not answer. The first officer asked "Why are you here?"

To this question, Mina had practiced her response. "I love Aamreeka. I came to my dreamland to visit my brother."

The man seemed satisfied and went through the second bag.

In a short time, Mina's clothes, books, and audio tapes spread out on the floor along with the *National*-brand rice cooker that Mother had sent for Hossein, her brother. Mina did not have much with her. She was not quite ready to leave when Hossein called and told her about the situation, but she could not afford to wait either. Her life would be ruined if Iran's Islamic government did not let her leave the country or the Americans stopped her from entering the U.S.

She had sold some of her belongings and left the rest to her sister Mahnaz. She kept only a few dresses, her favorite singer, Marzieh,'s audio tapes, some personal toiletries, and her books - the books Mohsen had demanded that she read. She had already had her bachelor's diploma translated, but she was unable to obtain transcripts for the master's level classes she had taken in the past two years. The University of Tehran and many other educational institutions had closed down months ago.

She had flown from Tehran to London on Iran Air, then to New York's JFK airport on British Airways. She was now supposed to fly from New York to Los Angeles on PanAm.

She had not even had time to say goodbye to Mohsen. She did not have his address or a telephone number and she could not find Zary either. She had last seen Zary the day the Muslim Students seized the US Embassy.

At 5:30, an hour past her flight's departure to LA, much to Mina's surprise, the younger officer stamped her passport and gave it back to her. He then left with the other officer.

Mina repacked her belongings and dragged her suitcases to a telephone booth near the office. She must call Hossein and ask him how to get another flight to Los Angeles. She had a couple of hundreds, tens, and one-dollar bills in her pocket. She held a few one-dollar bills in her hand and stood next to the telephone booth.

A young man was talking on the phone. When he

noticed her waiting, he quickly finished his call, and left the booth. With an apologetic smile, he said something to Mina. Mina held out her hand to him with the money. The young man looked at her with surprise.

"Please help me to tele-phone my brother in Los Angeles," Mina said while showing him the phone number in her small notebook and pointing to the telephone.

"Oh sorry, sorry. You need change to make a call to Los Angeles." The man took some quarters, dimes, and nickels out of his pocket and showed them to her. Mina gazed at him bashfully.

"Do you want me to help you make a phone call?" the young man asked.

"Yes, tanki you. Please, tanki you," Mina said in broken English.

The young man put a few coins into the box and dialed the number. Mina offered him the dollar bills again.

"No, thanks. I'm glad I could help," he said.

The man's red hair resembled those of the officer who had given her the visa at the Embassy two years ago. Mina wondered if he were among the hostages.

"Tanki you. Tanki you wery much," Mina said while she looked at him doubtfully.

Hossein wasn't at home. She left a message.

The handle of one of the suitcases broke when Mina pushed it to the side. She put the broken suitcase on top of the other and dragged them along.

Feeling extremely thirsty, she stopped at a small coffee shop. The word "Milk" on the beverage list caught her attention. She ordered a glass of milk and drank it all.

The airport was crowded and all the seats were occupied. Mina walked around twice before she found a vacant chair. She put down the heavy suitcases next to the chair. Exhausted, she collapsed.

Every once in awhile, the loudspeakers made different announcements, which Mina could not understand. A group of short, small-bodied men with almond shaped eyes, all wearing dark gray suits and each holding a camera, passed in front of her. An Indian woman, with a red bindi on her forehead and her belly button showing through her sari, held a little girl as she sat next to Mina.

Although she had not eaten since the night before, she did not feel hungry. The tight waist of her dress pushed on her stomach. She had spent more than twenty-four hours flying and waiting in London to connect with her next flight. She was not even drowsy. She only wanted to cry. She blinked hard to stop the tears, then rested her head on the chair and closed her eyes. Unable to sleep, she lifted one of her hands and caressed her stomach with the tip of her fingers. A moment later, Mina felt a faint subtle movement beneath her fingers; a tapping sensation right above her belly button. She opened her eyes and stared at her stomach in astonishment. This was the first time the baby had moved. She wanted to tell someone. The baby's moving! My baby, my baby's moving!

She turned toward the Indian woman, but the woman did not notice her move. On her other side, a large black woman leaned her head on the chair and snored. Mina had never seen a person so dark and so heavy. She rested her head again, closed her eyes, and resumed stroking her stomach. Would Mohsen touch her belly if he were there? Most likely not. He had even questioned whether the baby was his. From the moment he had heard about it, he insisted that she get rid of the baby. Maybe he was right. Maybe she should have. Tears trickled from her eyes, rolled down her cheek and chin, and then slowly dropped down to her belly.

Where were Mother and Mahnaz now? She already missed them. She even missed Borazjan and its sand-winds, and Maryam Aliabadi.

Borazjan

"Please, please, *please* take me with you; for God's sake take me with you, I swear to God I will always wear a clean uniform, please, for God's sake..." Maryam Aliabadi wept and begged when Mrs. Tashakori had pulled her out of the line.

She cried so vigorously and wholeheartedly that the other students begged on her behalf, too. Finally, their teacher, Miss Ahmadi, was moved and asked Mrs. Tashakori to pardon her, if for no other reason than Maryam being an outstanding student. Mina and Maryam had always competed for being the top student of the class.

For the past week, Mrs. Tashakori, the school principal, had repeatedly stressed the importance of wearing clean clothes on this day. Any student, who had

13

a filthy or worn-out uniform, was pulled out of line and left behind. Mrs. Tashakori personally oversaw the review process.

Everybody was excited to go to the only paved road in the town to greet Shahbanoo Farah, the Empress.

Mother had left home early in the morning. It was the first time Mina saw her go into public not wearing a *chador*. Not even a scarf covering her hair. Having on a beautiful black suit and a pair of white gloves, she looked charming. The gloves surprised the kids the most. They had no idea where she'd got them. Mother left in a car sent by the mayor to pick her and other distinguished ladies up and take them to the airport to welcome Shahbanoo.

Mrs. Tashakori finally gave up and sent Maryam to the bathroom with Soghra Khanum, the janitor, to clean her uniform and wash her face and hands. She then gave Maryam a new white plastic collar to wear. Maryam looked thrilled. No one in school loved Shahbanoo Farah as much as Maryam did. She had collected all Shahbanoo's pictures in her scrapbook.

After making sure everything was perfect, Mrs. Tashakori left school to join the wives of the city officials.

Although invited, Mrs. Pashaee did not go for the welcoming ceremony. She told Mother she would never go to a public place without wearing a chador. A woman in her fifties, she lived with her son Sergeant Pashaee and her grandson, Hamid.

Miss Ahmadi and the rest of the teachers accompanied their pupils to the main street, which had recently been named, "Sixth of Bahman," to commemorate the day of the Shah's Enghelab-e-Sefid,

White Revolution. They were all holding small three-colored flags of Iran, on the center of them a lion holding a sword, posed in front of a glorious ray of a shining sun.

When they finally got there at 9:00, the students from the boys' schools were already there. Mina saw Hossein, her brother, and Hamid among the high school boys. The girls moved into the rows in front of the boys, and the teachers scattered all around to keep an eye on them. Unlike the other days, none of the female teachers wore *chador* and the male teachers were in suits and ties, all cleanly shaven.

It was almost two o'clock in the afternoon when the procession of cars showed up. Two big American cars with tinted windows followed by Shahbanoo Farah's big black Cadillac followed by ten more cars.

Miss Ahmadi raised one of her arms, and as they had practiced for the past two weeks, the students started chanting:

Long live Pahlavi's dynasty,
Long live *Shahanshah*

The students shoved and pushed each other and poked their heads out of the lines to be the first to see Shahbanoo. While shouting at the students, the teachers equally excited also hurried into the street. SAVAK officers, wearing big dark sunglasses, howled at both the students and the teachers.

"Miss, Miss, go back to the sidewalk!"

"Hey… shoo, shoo, what is this manner? Why are you lowering your head like a mule and coming to the middle of the street? Go back to the lines! Who is responsible for these animals?"

"Hey Mister... Mister... I am talking to you moron! Where is your attention? Are you the one who is supposedly responsible for these donkeys?"

As Shahbanoo passed them, all the students ran alongside the car, crying:

Long live Pahlavi's dynasty,
Long live *Shahanshah*

The black Cadillac slowed down a short distance from them. Mina and Maryam were the closest to the car. Maryam also was the loudest of the crowd. Through the semi-dark windows of the car, Mina saw Mr. governor sitting in the back some distance away from Shahbanoo. When the car fully stopped, Mr. governor rushed out, ran around the car, opened the door for Shahbanoo, and bowed to her almost to his knees. Shahbanoo stepped out of the car gracefully; one foot first, then the other. Mina's heart pounded hard as Shahbanoo walked toward the lines, slowly and elegantly. She was tall—taller than many men around, and taller than any woman Mina had ever seen.

Officials hurried toward her. Mr. Tashakori, the director of education, Mrs. Tashakori's husband, arrived after the others, breathing hard. He grabbed Shahbanoo's hand, bowing and kissing it with a loud noise.

Long live Pahlavi's dynasty,
Long live Pahlavi's...

For a couple of seconds Shahbanoo waived to the students. Then she left to go unveil the Shah's statue, a new bronze sculpture installed in the middle of the square in front of the city hall.

As the cars disappeared, Mina could barely breathe, her throat dry from shouting and thirst. She could not believe it, she had seen Shahbanoo Farah in person! She had even seen Shahbanoo's big feet in her short-heeled shoes. She was so close that Mina could almost feel her smooth skin and see her high cheekbones and long delicate fingers. Her round black leather hat matched her shoes and purse. Her yellow suit resembled the color of sunflowers.

Maryam's uniform was torn in places, her white collar lost, and her face and hands much dirtier now than the morning. Although Mina had not been able to see Shahbanoo's eyes behind her big dark sunglasses, Maryam swore to God she had seen Shahbanoo's eyes looking at her. She wept, remembering Shahbanoo watching her when she said to her 'I love you.'

It was not until the following year that Mina and Mahnaz saw Mother wearing the same suit with no chador. She and other elite women of Borazjan were going to the mayor's office to vote for their congressional representative, which was a result of the extension of the Right to Vote to Women, one of the social reforms resulting from the White Revolution.

• • •

The next day, Nane-ye Mohammad, the mother of Mohammad, Mina's family housekeeper constantly prayed and thanked Shahbanoo. Around noon, big trucks had distributed blankets, clothes, and medicine among the poor people. Nane-ye Mohammad, and her

17

son, Mohammad, had gone back to the trucks several times until they were able to get two blankets, some medicine, and a jacket for Mohamad. Later that evening, she went around and told everyone she was most grateful for the medicine and ointments. She showed them to different people to find out which one was best for itching. She wanted them for her daughter, Zahra, who suffered from large black ticks deep down in her skin. Zahra scratched herself constantly until her skin started to bleed. Mina had seen Zahra for the first time the day Mother had sent her to Nane-ye Mohammad's house.

• • •

The gate was open. Mina entered a small dirt yard with one mudroom on each side. She didn't know which room was Nane-ye Mohammad's. She knew that the three of them, she, Mohammad, and Zahra, lived in only one room. She chose to go to the closer one.

"Nane-ye Mohammad... Nane-ye Mohammad!" No answer.

The room on the other side seemed empty. Still, Mina knocked on the door. "Nane-ye Mohammad, Nane-ye Mohammad!" No answer.

She waited a few seconds, then pushed the door open. The smoke and the smell of sheep dung struck her. The place was so murky she could hardly see, but she could hear the sounds of sheep and goats. The mud walls were almost black and the floor was made of dirt. Soon, a goat, two sheep, and another four-legged creature, smaller than the other animals, came along. She moved back. It is an animal pen, she thought. Before leaving, her eyes met the creature's face. It was smiling. A small girl! She smiled again. Her matted, dirt-covered hair was the color of hay. Green thick mucus hung from her nose. Her face was so dirty Mina thought she was a colored person. She said her name was Zahra.

Right after the New Year holidays of Nowruz, Zahra started to show up on Mina's way to school. Mina and Maryam lived in the same block and walked to school together.

Zahra wore two unmatched torn plastic sandals on her hands. They were different sizes and colors: one hot pink, the other lettuce green. Two thick rags wrapped around her knees.

As she saw the girls coming, she crawled quickly forward on her knees and hands to greet them. She sat in front of them with her arms supporting her body, her legs bent, lagging behind her.

Maryam burst into a laugh, "Hey, look at that seal!"

Mina hardly controlled her laughter. She felt deeply sorry for Zahra and tried to look serious but Maryam was right. Zahra looked like a seal in a picture Mina had shown her.

Mina and Maryam said hello to Zahra and walked away. Zahra followed them all the way to school without uttering a word.

When Mina and Maryam entered the school, Zahra stayed there motionless and stared at them until they had disappeared from her sight.

The next day, when they saw Zahra waiting for them, they changed their path, taking a different route to school. Zahra was smart. Shortly, she realized she should not show herself too soon. She would hide against a wall waiting for them to pass. When she was sure they could not change their path, she appeared and followed them all the way.

Sometimes Zahra would show up every day. Other times she would not come for a while. It mostly depended on the weather. If it was not too cold or too hot, or if the sand-wind was not blowing, she was there.

Her small hazel eyes and innocent smile resembled her brother's, Mohammad.

• • •

Mohammad worked in a shoe repair shop in a corner of the Bazaar. He had worked there since he was seven. At first, he just swept the shop, made tea for the crippled owner, and cleaned the mud and dirt from shoes with a damp cloth before the owner polished them. Now after three years of work, he had learned his job and polished shoes better than his master. He put even more shine on Father's shoes, which Mina took to him every week. One time he repaired the holes in the sole of Mahnaz's shoes and fixed the damaged leather of Mina's shoes, while Mina and Mahnaz waited in the shop. He worked faster and more wholeheartedly when Mahnaz was present. Mina teased Mahnaz and called her Nane-ye Mohammad's daughter-in-law. It made Mahnaz so upset that she screamed, cried, and complained to Mother every time. Mother would chase Mina, and if she caught her, she would hit her with her hookah's pipe, but not too hard to hurt her.

Mohammad's small body looked even smaller in the

brown medium-sized man's jacket that was the plunder of his last visit to the drug-and-food distribution trucks after Shahbanoo's visit. The jacket would be too big for him even in five years.

He told everybody the details of how he got the jacket, embellishing the story while bragging about it in front of Mina and Mahnaz who listened to him with curiosity and interest.

On his first trip to the trucks, he gained a big sack of rice, on the second, a blanket. On his third visit, he noticed the jackets. He absolutely needed one.

"A huge gypsy fella, big as a giant, stood in front of me. We both reached for the jackets, but his arms were longer than mine, and he snatched the last one before I could. I begged the officer to give me one too, but he didn't have any more. When I kept begging he got angry and wanted to beat me up, but I jumped back. I was really pissed off. The gypsy giant was leaving with my jacket to go back to his tent. I followed him for three blocks. After he passed the Police Department and turned into the alley behind the big prison, I grabbed the jacket and ran away."

Mohammad had not returned home all day in case someone followed him. The gypsy had been a good choice. Gypsies would stay in town for a short time, leaving when it became too warm and not returning until the following year.

Mina thought the drugs and jackets were gifts from America.

• • •

From behind the dust-covered windows, the fifth graders could see the steam rising from the boiling milk. They could hardly concentrate on Miss Ahmadi's instruction; they all waited for a knock on the door to let them know it was their turn to get their portion of daily milk.

When Soghra Khanum finally knocked, the students rushed out without waiting for Miss Ahmadi's permission. They went toward the table in the middle of the schoolyard and formed a long line in front of it. Mina blew on her bare hands to keep them warm.

Mrs. Tashakori's twins stayed on the other side of the yard talking with their friends, mostly non-locals. Every year at the beginning of the milk distribution, Mina stayed with them and ignored the milk too, but as the weather grew colder, she gave up. She cupped her hands around the glass and warmed them with its heat.

A couple of months before Nowruz, the Department of Education sent powdered milk to schools. The word "Milk," inscribed on the boxes, was the only English word everyone knew well. Miss Ahmadi could read the smaller words: "Made in America."

"In *Aamrika,* kids drink a glass of milk every day," said Mrs. Tashakori on the first day of milk distribution. "The President of America Mr. Kennedy, sends these milks to poor countries so that their children have milk, too." Before the speech was over, the girls were running to the other side of the yard to line up for the hot milk.

• • •

Mrs. Tashakori came out of her office and stood by

the door. She usually came to school late, unless there was an important matter. Everyone in the yard began mumbling. She stayed there until two of the teachers pulled up the flag and the students finished reciting the "Imperial Salute of Iran", the national anthem:

Long live the Shah, our king of Kings,
And may his glory make immortal our land...

Then she came closer and stood next to the flag. She could see everybody from there; the schoolyard was three steps below her. She wore a print dress with little flowers over her pudgy body and her wavy black hair covered her short plump neck.

Mina nervously looked at her fingernails. Thank God, they were clean and short. She touched her recently washed white collar, now slightly turned darker. There was no danger. The last time Mrs. Tashakori passed by the lines, she had a couple of students smacked with a wooden ruler, ten times on each hand. One had acted too mischievously, three had long fingernails with dirt under them, and one had a dirty collar.

Mrs. Tashakori had come with her family to Borazjan from the north western city of Tabriz at the beginning of the last school year. She had a strange heavy accent, different from the students and the teachers. Her twins were   Mina and Maryam's classmates. They spoke with each other in Turkish so no one could understand them.

The students stood still in the lines, while Mrs. Tashakori read from a printout she held in her hands:

"Yesterday, in the state of Texas, in the country of America, there was a shooting against Mr. John

Fitzgerald Kennedy, the President of the United States of America. The doctors' efforts to save him were not effective and he died after a few hours in front of his wife, Mrs. Jacqueline, and his two young children, John and Carolyn."

Once again, the yard filled with whispers and mumbling. Many of the students did not know about whom she was talking. Maryam Aliabadi, standing in the line in front of Mina, mimicked Mrs. Tashakori in a hushed voice:

"John Fitzz!"

"Fittzz!"

She pronounced the "i" very fast, put emphasis on the letter "t", and said the "z" faster and louder. Everybody around her laughed quietly. Mina controled her giggles. Miss Ahmadi looked at them sternly from above the steps, and put her forefinger to her lips to quiet them.

Even Mina, who read every article, newspaper, and magazine she could get her hands on, and had read some articles about the Kennedy family, had not known Mr. Kennedy's middle name was Fitzgerald.

Some of Mina's friends, whose fathers were the directors of various offices, spent their summer vacation in Tehran and came back to Borazjan when schools opened in the fall. The girls usually brought her magazines that she could not find in Borazjan. A year before, when the Shah *and* Shahbanoo Farah had traveled to America, she had seen some pictures of president Kennedy and his wife Jacqueline standing next to the Shah and Shahbanoo. In one picture, Shahbanoo wore a big white hat while Jacqueline

Kennedy had a smaller one on. Everybody agreed that Shahbanoo's hat was much prettier and more glamorous than Jacqueline's. The Shah did not look as handsome as Kennedy, who had blue eyes and blond hair. In one picture, the Shah's eyes fixed on Mina's no matter which angle Mina chose to look at him.

In a less confident tone of voice, Mrs. Tashakori then announced, "Now, in memory of Mr. Kennedy, we will all hold a moment of silence."

All students looked at each other in surprise. A moment of silence for a dead person? She must be kidding. But Mrs. Tashakori's face was serious.

"Is everybody ready?" She looked around again. "Let's start," she said, gazing at her wristwatch.

The students had trouble staying still. They looked at each other from under their eyelids. Maryam tightened her mouth hard, looking down, tried not to explode into laughter. Oh, what a long minute! Mina could hardly wait; she wanted to ask someone why silence? You should cry for mourning; you should slap your face and your chest; you should wail and wear black; and you should not enjoy anything or laugh for a long time, the way mother had mourned grandfather's death. He had died during his pilgrimage to Karbala, when Mina was only six years old.

"The one-minute-silence is an American ritual. It was written in the ordinance from Tehran," Miss Ahmadi explained when Mina asked later on. "The government had ordered all schools declare a minute of silence for Mr. Kennedy during their morning ceremony."

It seemed all the mysteries came from Tehran. Mina

25

always had numerous questions from the girls coming back from Tehran. How long did it take you to get to Tehran? How many cars are on Tehran's streets? What models? Are they all new? How long does it take to go from one side of the city to the other? Wow... two hours with a car! How many cinemas does it have? Television? What is television?

"A big radio. You can see the newscaster while you listen to him talking, and you can see movies on it instead of going to a cinema."

Did you go to Lalezaar? How about Toopkhaneh's Square? Are all the women no longer wearing chador? Where did you buy that shiny leather bag? Where is the Berlin Alley? Oh...yeah, I know, in Lalezaar, you've told me about it before. It is where you buy your shoes and stockings.

Mina gave the Tehrani girls all her savings to buy her translated paperback novels from Tehran. The books she could never find in Borazjan. Europeans, Americans, Russians, she liked them all. Rebecca by Daphne Du Maurier, The Feather by Matheson, Tobacco Road by Erskine Caldwell, Brothers Karamazov by Dostoyevsky, For Whom the Bell Tolls by Hemingway.

Her dreams of visiting the city became a reality when, right after her graduation from elementary school, Father took them to Tehran and then to the North for summer vacation.

Caspian Sea

Aug. 1964 / Mordad 1343

Mina could never forget that night, the night she and Mahnaz stayed up until dawn, marking their trip from Borazjan to the North on a map. Hossein was as excited as they were.

Mina had an atlas with a foldout map of Iran. She brought the book to bed and they marked their trip in red. They would cross almost the entire length of Iran; from Borazjan, near Bushehr at the shore of the Persian Gulf to the Caspian Sea in the north, the world's largest saltwater lake. A lake so big they called it a sea. A sea sitting on the back of that cat, the map of Iran.

On the way to Tehran, they would pass Shiraz, Esfahan and Qom. Mother had always wanted to go to

Qom on a pilgrimage to the shrine of her holiness Masoumeh, the granddaughter of the Prophet, and the sister of martyr Imam Hossein. From Tehran, they were to go to the North. Father had not said to which city in the North. He just promised to take them to a place with lots of forests and beaches, a place where women went swimming naked, wearing only bathing suits.

The next day, all their classmates knew about the upcoming trip.

The school closed in the middle of June, but Father's request for a two-week vacation had not been approved yet. At the end of the month, Father agreed that Mother, Mina and Mahnaz go to Shiraz where Mother's family lived, and wait for Father and Hossein to come.

Mina had never waited for, or missed, Father so badly.

In the middle of July, Father, not wanting to wait any longer, joined them in Shiraz along with Ali Agha. Mr. Ali was Nane-ye Mohammad's brother-in-law and an experienced truck driver on the roads between Borazjan and Shiraz.

Father did not know how to drive; yet, with a special loan from work, he had recently bought a small blue Russian Moskovich. The car was only five years old, but looked, and felt, much older. It was parked in front of their home, and Father asked anyone who knew how to drive, to give them a lift in it.

Morteza, Uncle Ahmad's eldest son, who was Hossein's age, accompanied them on the trip. Ali Agha sat in the driver seat with Father and Morteza taking the passenger side; Mother sat in the backseat, with Mina, Mahnaz and Hossein. Although it was an eight-hour drive from Shiraz to Esfahan, they drove straight there. They stopped only to get gas, to eat lunch, and for Mother and Ali Agha to recite their daily prayers.

Father had a cousin in Esfahan, whom none of the children had ever met. They spent the night at his house. Father and his cousin did not sleep that night. They went to the "Society of Retired Army Officers" to play poker. Father was an obsessive gambler who played poker at least two nights a week. At dawn, he and his cousin came home with a big pot of *kalleh pacheh*. Having won the night before, he was very happy, and later when they went to visit the city, he bought *gaz* and other delightful treats for them. He also bought a pair of earrings for Mina, a necklace for Mahnaz and a picture frame for Mother; engraved with images of the historical Si-o-Se-Pol bridge and Menar-Jomban tower.

In Qom, Mother changed her chador to go to visit the shrine and pay her respect to her holiness Masoumeh. Mother had brought three chadors with her. A black *crêpe* for holy places; a light casual chador with small prints to wear on the way; and a fancy black-and-white polka-dot one. She had made the last one especially for this trip. Mina and Mahnaz liked the dotted one the most. Mother looked so pretty in it. She was saving it to wear in Tehran and the North.

Mina and Father did not go to the shrine with others. Mina stayed in the car to read her book, The Razor's Edge, which she brought from Esfahan. She had seen the book on a shelf in the living room of Mr. Fazilat, her father's cousin, and started to read it there. Mr. Fazilat had lent her the book to finish on the way. Mina was not sure how to pronounce the writer's name Somerset

Maugham. Neither father nor Mr. Fazilat knew. In Farsi, Somerset could be pronounced both Summer-set and Summ-rest. It was confusing. The book amused Mina. What a great journey. Larry, the protagonist, had abandoned his wealthy family to travel to India in search of an entirely new life.

In Tehran, they stayed at the hotel Sedaghat_e No, The New Honesty Hotel on Rah Ahan, the Rail Road, Square. The hotel was on the corner of a small alley and above a row of grocery stores, bakeries, vegetable stores, and gift shops. Father knew the owner, Teimur Khan, and his wife, Miss Iran, from before.

They climbed a narrow staircase to a passage with the streets on one side and the office and rooms on the other. Teimur Khan was not in the office. Iran Khanum sat at a dirty desk in the corner of the room and talked with two older men in poor, broken Arabic. Numerous papers, a tea flask, and a few teacups and saucers covered the desk.

After recognizing Father, Iran Khanum sent her son, Bahram, to inform his father of their arrival. Bahram was the same age as Hossein and Morteza. After greeting them, Teimur Khan checked the hotel's log and gave them the best available room. Azar, their daughter, took them to a large room with two twin-sized bronze beds and a cement floor covered with an old Persian rug and a couple of blankets. Azar and Bahram worked in the hotel all summer helping their parents.

The hallways were full of children playing and making noise. The scent of cooking and exotic spices drifted from the open windows of the rooms all day. Mina heard loud voices speaking Arabic, Kurdish,

Turkish, Gilaki, and Farsi with accents that sounded strange to her ear.

Mina and Mahnaz stood in the balcony, leaning on the fence, watched the street for hours. The crowded Rah Ahan Square and the honking of cars stunned Mina. The pedestrians passed through the busy street, not paying attention to the cars or the complaints of drivers. Hossein and Morteza joined them sometimes. None of them had ever seen so many cars and people in the same place.

Some evenings Mina, Mahnaz, Hossein, and Morteza went to the rooftop of the hotel with Azar and Bahram, and through the dusty windows of a neighbor's family room watched a box called television. Although they could not clearly see the moving pictures on the box or hear the sound, Mina loved it all. How life was different here. Mina even loved the Tehrani accent - the way they pronounced sentences so quickly, the charming timbre of their voices. When she returned home, although she had not been in Tehran for even a week, she tried to imitate Azar and Bahram's accent. She would say words faster and change the place of vowels in some words to make them sound more cosmopolitan. Other girls made fun of her and mimicked her funny way of talking. She did not mind it until she herself got tired of the game and went back to her old dialect, a mix of her mother's Shirazi accent and Borazjani.

Mina and Mahnaz were most eager to see Lalezaar Street and Berlin Alley. They had both saved their Nowruz money to buy white-laced collars and ankle-length stockings.

● ● ●

It took them over an hour to drive from Rah Ahan Square to Lalezaar. They passed Amirieh, Monirieh, Ferdowsi Square and Ferdowsi Street. Then they continued in Istanbul Street until they reached Lalezaar. Downtown, the streets were cleaner, brighter, and not as noisy as Rah Ahan Square. Some of the multi-story buildings had dark mysterious looking windows while others were clean and well lit.

Parking a car in Lalezaar was a frustrating task; Ali Agha was not used to parking in a small space. Three ragged boys stood on the side of street, mocking and laughing at him. The boys did not look like Tehranis at all. Embarrassed, Ali Agha hit the car in front of him and the one behind him several times until he managed to park.

The street was quite busy. It was a long walk to Berlin Alley. Father, Hossein, and Morteza walked faster, ahead of others. Mother, holding Mina and Mahnaz's hands, followed them. She was amazed by the store windows as much as Mina and Mahnaz. Ali Agha, uncomfortable, walked dreamingly behind them.

Both sides of Lalezaar were lined with gift shops, shoe and clothing stores. Mother stopped a couple of times to look at the mannequins in the store windows. The mannequins wore black, blond, and brown wigs, and colorful dresses, their sightless gazes lost in the window spaces. Cinemas and theaters popped up occasionally. The most spectacular was the Nasr Theater, its windows covered with photos of actors and actresses in different poses. In the middle of one window, there was a photo of a belly dancer, wearing a glittering long skirt and a bra. She held a dazzling red scarf in front of her lower face and gazed at people. In another photo, she was dressed in a Panama hat and a very short skirt; her big bosom peeked at them through her open V-neck blouse. She held the two ends of a scarf hanging from the sides of her neck.

The caption above the photos read, "Tonight, and every night, with the legendary dancer, bride of the Orient, Madam Jamileh."

Father bought two tickets for Morteza and Hossein to see the show. They were so excited that they left the group and went in without even saying goodbye. Mina and Mahnaz begged Mother to allow them to accompany the boys. Mother did not approve. Father and Ali Agha had seen the show the night before.

As they got closer to Berlin Alley, the street grew more crowded and busy. There was a huge fabric store on one corner of the intersection of Berlin Alley and Lalezaar and another enormous garment store on the other corner. This store alone was larger than all of Borazjan's garment stores together. A beautiful mannequin with blue eyes and blond hair stood in one of the windows. She wore a bridal gown with a long lace skirt and a satin sleeveless top. Her shoulders were naked. She had a pair of long white gloves on, covering her hands and arms up above her elbows. Mina and Mahnaz were overwhelmed watching the bride. Their reflections appeared on each side of the bride in the clean glass of the window. Mahnaz, astonished, went in to see the back of the mannequin.

Mother   panicked   when   she   noticed   her

33

disappearance and started to shout at Mina. She had told them all the way they should not move from her side. Tehran was not like Borazjan. There were all kinds of people there; thieves, murderers, and junkies. Sergeant Pashaee's mother had told her never to leave the girls alone on the streets of Tehran. They would be stolen and sold out to the whorehouses. There was a big brothel called 'The Castle,' which was full of kidnapped or naive girls from all over the country. Mina went into the store and fetched Mahnaz. Mother was so angry that she smacked them both. Mahnaz started crying. Mina tried hard not to cry in front of strangers. Mother grabbed their hands and walked faster. They couldn't find Father.

Further down, in the middle of the alley, a group of women and young girls, had gathered around a table full of garments. A not-so-young-man clapped his hands, and with a loud voice, invited everybody to buy something. Mahnaz pulled her hand away from Mother and ran toward him. Mina followed her and grabbed her hand. On the table, among the garments, was a big cardboard sign, inscribed with large black ink letters "Agha Seyed Jalaal Yek Kalam." A tall, big-bellied man stood on top of the table clapping harder and hollering passionately.

"Don't miss this once in a lifetime opportunity! Everything must go! Come! Come closer ladies. Come and get one of these colorful ones! I carry all sizes. Come closer, you young lady! Super Sale! Super Sale! Everything half off! Only five tomans each. You can't buy it for less than ten tomans in the stores."

He jumped down from the table, selected two of the

smaller shirts, and offered them to Mother. "It is almost free, free, only ten tomans for two. You cannot find this price anywhere. Agha Seyed Jalal Yek kalam is giving it away!"

Mina and Mahnaz looked at Mother with pleading eyes. Mother smiled at the man and shyly walked away, dragging them along. Further down, they found Father and Ali Agha in front of a sandwich shop, waiting for them to have dinner together.

When they returned to the Theater to pick up Morteza and Hossein, daylight was gone, but the many neon lights above the stores and cinemas illuminated the street, and it was even more crowded than before.

• • •

Father took them to the northern part of Tehran the day before they left for the North. They drove almost the whole length of Pahlavi Street, and just before turning toward the mountains and arriving in Tajrish Square, they saw a young girl, the same age as Mahnaz, riding a bike. Ali agha slowed down the car and everybody scrutinized her. She wore a pair of blue shorts - almost ten centimeters above her knees, and a printed white and blue sleeveless shirt. As they passed her, Mother, Mina and Mahnaz, turned their heads and watched her until she disappeared from sight. Mother called to God, *b-ismi-llāhi r-raḥmāni r-raḥīmi*, in the name of Allah, the most gracious, the most merciful. Ali Agha said loudly, "God saves us. The day of resurrection is coming soon. Girls coming to the streets wearing shorts!"

When they returned to the hotel and told Teimur

Khan about the girl in the shorts, he laughed and said, "There are lots of these Mademoiselles in uptown."

That evening, Mother borrowed a frying pan and a small Primus stove from Iran Khanum. She fried up various kinds of *kuku* to take with them for the rest of their trip. Father had bought the ingredients from the shops below the hotel, but he had forgotten the frying oil. Mother asked Mina to get some from the people in the room next door. They were a big family on a pilgrimage to Mashhad and the holy shrine of Imam Reza. Mother dreamed of going to Mashhad someday to pay her respect to Imam Reza, her most beloved Imam.

An old woman opened the door. She wore a fine white scarf and a long loose dress over baggy pants. She had a blue tattooed beauty mark between her eyebrows and wore lots of *sormeh* around her eyes. She gave Mina a half-empty-tin of shortening.

● ● ●

The next day, after Ali Agha said his sunrise prayer, they left Tehran for the North. After two hours of driving, they came to a coffeehouse in a beautiful grove of lush trees by a river. Father asked Ali Agha to stop and they got out. They sat at a big wooden table under a tall green maple tree. Mother, Mina and Mahnaz put *kuku*, *lavash*, feta cheese, and unshelled walnuts on the table. Father ordered seven cups of tea and three fried eggs to keep the owner happy.

The boys went to the river to play. Ali Agha washed his face and hands to prepare for noon prayer, in case he didn't find more running water before then.

After the meal, Mother stretched her legs and let her chador fall to her shoulders. The weather was chilly; nevertheless Mina enjoyed it. At that time of the year, in Borazjan and the South, the weather was so hot that, as Mother put it, "It was as if fire was blowing from the sky and the earth." Mahnaz sat close to Mother and leaned back on her, feeling the warmth of her body. Mother put her arms around her, and with a smile she said to Father, "This is the heaven they talk about!"

"You haven't seen the rest of it! I am taking you somewhere for lunch, somewhere you've never imagined!" Father responded.

Mina was sure Father had not seen the place either; otherwise he would have talked about it all the way. Someone in Tehran must have told him about it.

Unlike the roads from Borazjan to Shiraz, or from Shiraz to Tehran, where they drove several hours before seeing a decent place; on the way north there were many places to tempt them to make a stop.

Father seemed very pleased and cheerful. A few times, he had Ali Agha pull the car in front of a soda stand, and he bought them Pepsi, Canada Dry, and Oso. The road was beautiful; paved and straight. It was nothing like the winding dirt roads of the South. Along the road there were pastures and meadows. Once in a while, a cow would cross the road. The first time it happened, Father put his head out and shouted "Mademoiselle, be careful, you might get hit by a car!" They all laughed. The second time they saw a cow, Ali Agha shouted "Boss, another madmoosl!" They all laughed again. Father had learned the word "mademoiselle" from Teimur Khan.

An hour past noon they saw the first sign, "Motel Qoo – 5 kilometers." Father extended his right arm and dramatically announced, "Motel Qoo. The place I am taking you all for lunch and a rest!" His eyes sparkled.

Mother took off the casual chador, folded it, and put it in her handbag. Then, she got out her polka-dot one. After unfolding a layer, she smoothed out the creases, and then unfolded another. When the chador was completely unfolded, she put it on. Mahnaz helped her draw a lock of hair from under the chador, and gave it a beautiful curl, the way Mother liked it. Mother looked very pretty this way.

With each kilometer, all the children announced the remaining distance to Motel Qoo. With one kilometer remaining, they began counting aloud to make the time go faster. One, two, three... forty-five, forty-six...four hundred... Five hundred, five hundred and one, five hundred and two...

A big metal arch appeared. Motel Qoo.

Ali Agha drove under the Motel Qoo's sign and into a big parking lot. Their car fit easily between two big new cars, one black, the other blue.

Father, Morteza and Ali agha got out, and then Father let the rest of them out of the back. Mina jumped out so quickly that her foot got stuck on the edge of the door and she tripped. Mother grabbed her and yelled, "Why are you in such a hurry? You should be more ladylike!"

Ali Agha walked around one of the cars beside theirs: "Boss, it is a Buick!"

Father looked at the car and said in a respectful tone, "It is American. American cars are the best!"

They walked toward the motel, passing the smaller buildings. Mina was the first to see the restaurant and, just beyond it, the sea. Men, women, and children were in bathing suits. Some were walking around on the shimmering sand, while others lay on bright towels under colorful umbrellas. It was the first time Mina had seen women in bathing suits, though she'd seen pictures in magazines. The water of the Caspian Sea was much bluer than the water of the Persian Gulf, the weather not as hot and humid. Mina was completely entranced.

Ahead of them, two men, two women, and three children entered the restaurant. One of the women wore a sleeveless tailored green dress with hot pink flowers. The children, two boys and a girl wore bathing suits. The girl, who looked the same age as Mina, wore colorful sandals and her toenails were polished bright red. Mina nearly hid behind Mother.

Mina had on a brown-and-beige plaid jumper with a long-sleeved red blouse underneath. The heels of her black shoes were worn out and the tips had faded. Mahnaz wore a navy blue dress which Mother made for her. Her hair was tied back with a thick brown elastic ponytail holder.

Father and Ali Agha led the way and entered the restaurant, followed by Mother, whose polka-dot chador was open in the front. Hossein, Morteza, Mina, and Mahnaz walked behind them.

A waiter in a black suit, white shirt, and red-and-blue tie stood taking orders. Another waiter, dressed in the same uniform, was carrying a tray of meals and sodas to another table. Two busboys were taking the empty dishes to the kitchen.

The maître d', a salt-and-pepper-haired man, sat behind a podium talking to a waiter, giving him orders about the people who had arrived just before them. As soon as the maître d' saw them, he came out from behind his podium and addressed Father, "Ladies are not allowed to enter the restaurant wearing a chador."

Father looked at Mother and at the others, then turned to maître d' and, with a modest smile, said, "A white-dotted chador isn't a real chador!" He laughed a bit, and they all laughed with him. The maître d' looked irritated and said, "The rule stands." Then he went back to his podium.

Now, Father got angry. He began to shout. He looked at Mother and continued shouting. Mina's gaze moved between Mother and Father. Mother turned pale and hid more in her chador. Everyone turned and stared at them. Mina blushed, and lowered her eyes. The three kids, who had entered the restaurant right before them, got up from their chairs and walked over to stand in front of Mina and Mahnaz. Two other small girls followed them. One of the girls stared at Mina's outfit and whispering to the other girl, they began to giggle.

Two waiters came forward. With the maître d', they backed them out of the restaurant.

Ali Agha was too panicked to say a word.

"You son of bitches," Father cried. "You have no shame! Preventing a covered woman from entering a restaurant in an Islamic country!"

Then in a voice only they could hear, he said, "They think we're still in the period of Reza *Qoldor*." He yelled at Mother, "Missus, how many times do I need to tell you not to dress like a house servant?"

"If I knew they would throw us out because of my chador, I would have done something about it," Mother said while lowering the top of her chador to her forehead. Her bang could not be seen anymore.

Mahnaz took Mother's hand as Father angrily walked away. They followed him to the car. Mina had never seen him so angry. She couldn't believe he had actually said "Reza Qoldor," Reza the Bully was the insulting name people had called the Shah's father, the old Shah, when he had ordered police to use force to take away all chadors worn by women in public.

Ali Agha turned the ignition, but the car didn't start. He tried again, and the car made a crowing sound and stopped. No one spoke except Father, who cursed continuously. "You motherfuckers. I will fuck your mothers and sisters. I know what to do with you sons of bitches. Let me get back to Tehran. I will go straight to the Ministry of Justice. I will go directly to the minister. How dare you? How dare you stop a Muslim woman from entering a restaurant? I will fuck your sisters."

Then he yelled at Ali Agha who, in embarrassment and confusion, repeatedly pushed the gas pedal and turned the ignition. Ali Agha got out, pulled a metal crank out of the trunk, and cranked the engine at the front of the car. It started and then stopped. Mina was about to burst into tears.

Finally the engine started. Ali agha jumped in and backed out from between the two big American Buicks. They left Motel Qoo, their car thumping like a hammer on a copper pot, with smoke trailing behind them.

After having a quick lunch at a Kebab shop by the roadside, they started back toward Borazjan. They didn't even stop in Tehran; Father was too embarrassed to tell Teimur Khan and Iran Khanum what had happened in Motel Qoo.

When they passed Isfahan, Mina pulled out the pages of The Razor's Edge and let them blow away out of the window. She kept her mind busy with the upcoming years of high school.

• • •

I *am*, you *are*, she *is*, I *was*, you *were*...

Mina loved the English lessons. Reading from left to right and learning the 'to be' verbs was fun. They changed with each subject. Mina was in the backroom studying. High school was more engaging.

It was the tenth day of Nowruz. The New Year's visitations were all done, with only three days left to *sizdah bedar*, the thirteenth day of the year, and the end of the school break. Mother was taking her afternoon nap. Hossein and Father were not home, and Mahnaz played with their small kittens; a white one with black paws and two orange ones with black and gray striped lines. Mina wished she, too, could play with the kittens, but her homework was more important.

Two short hesitant knocks on the gate. Mahnaz ran to the door. "It's Hamid!"

Mina's heart started pounding. She headed to the gate too. Before she reached the door, she heard Mahnaz's voice again: "Hossein's not home, he's gone to play soccer."

Mina rushed to the door and stood behind Mahnaz so that Hamid could see her. Hamid pushed the gate open and held out his hand, offering something to Mina.

"I went hunting with my uncle yesterday," his voice trembled. "I shot these myself."

Mahnaz jumped back. Mina looked at Hamid's gift curiously. He held up three small slaughtered birds skewered on thin wooden sticks; their headless neck and tiny legs hung from the sides, all plucked. "These are sparrows." He blushed.

The birds looked like the bats flying at night in between wood planks of their ceiling. Mahnaz, now excited, stretched one arm to take the sparrows. Mina jumped forward and grabbed them.

"Thanks," she said quickly and ran back inside.

The prior year, Hamid had come from Kurdistan to live with his uncle and grandmother. They talked Kurdish with each other, a language Mina could not understand. He was in the same class as Hossein. Very soon they became closest friends and fellow soccer players. Sergeant Pashaee brought Hamid with him when he came to play card with Father.

Hamid and Hossein watched every movie shown in Borazjan's only cinema together. When there was an American Western, they went every night. Hamid gathered the film negatives the projectionist cut and threw away. He kept a collection of pictures of American artists.

Mother took Mina or Mahnaz with her when she went to see Mrs. Pashaee. Mina carried her school books with her to have excuse to get help from Hamid on her homework, but Hamid stayed in his room while they were there. If his grandmother called him to do something, he lowered his head, did the task, and went back to his room. Although Hamid never looked at Mina directly, she knew he was always aware of her presence and watched her whenever she was looking away.

Most mornings Hamid came to pick up Hossein for school. Their house was not on Hamid's way to school, but he often waited for Hossein at the corner with his bicycle when Mina left for school.

His bicycle was nicer than anyone else's in the neighborhood. It had a black horn on each handle and one red bulb installed on the rim of each wheel. As Hamid pedaled, the bulbs lit up and turned along with the wheels. Hossein sat on the back seat and held Hamid's jacket, and they went to school together. Mina stood and watched until they were out of sight.

A year later Mina discovered why Hamid had moved to Borazjan.

● ● ●

'Colonel Pashaee, Hamid's father is in jail."
"What? Why?"
"He had killed his wife, Hamid's mother."
Mina learned these through hushed conversations, stealthy weeping and whisperings between Mother and Mrs. Pashaee.

One night, when Colonel Pashaee, Hamid's father, had unexpectedly returned home from a military mission, he found a stranger in bed with his wife. He immediately took out his revolver and shot them both. He got five years for killing his wife's lover, but nothing for killing her. Killing his wife was not a crime; he had only defended his honor.

The following year Colonel Pashaee was released from prison and Hamid was sent back to Sanandaj in Kurdistan to live with him.

Hamid never came back and never got in touch with Hossein again. Years later, they heard Hamid had gone to America, staying with his aunt and going to college there.

Mina's Revolution

Tehran - University

June 1970 / Khordad 1348

"Tehran? Are you out of your mind?' Father sounded like this was the first time he heard Mina talking about Tehran. "Who ever heard of a girl going to Tehran and living there alone? You wouldn't be safe in that crazy, filthy environment even if you were a man." He grabbed one of Mina's magazines and threw it out of the door into their partially cemented yard. "Haven't you read about all those terrible stories in your magazines? It was just in the last issue you brought home, a long article about how they trick girls; get them addicted to drugs, and then make them do a thousand bad things."

"I am not one of those stupid girls!" Mina shouted.

"Yes, sure you are a smart girl, but, a *girl* is a *girl*. You cannot let a girl be alone," Mother said. "A girl should lay her head where her mother's head is, or there will be much gossip about her. If you go to Tehran, no honor would be left for us in this town."

Mina tried to be calm, "I just want to go to the University of Tehran. I will be back right after finishing my studies."

"No, no, no!" Father's face and neck were red now. "Student or no student, it doesn't matter. If you live in a filthy environment like Tehran you would become rotten."

"Tell me why you have to go to the University of Tehran to study? Aren't there any other universities closer to us?"

Father wanted her to go to the Academy of Teachers in Bushehr, just two hours away: "But only on one condition. You have to stay in the girl's dorm. You will come home directly Thursdays after school, and I will take you back to Bushehr on Saturday mornings."

"Let her go to Shiraz to study nursing or midwifery. She can go to Pahlavi University. Midwifery is a fitting job for a girl. She can find a job here easily. Mina is a clever girl; she can support herself and become somebody. In Shiraz, she can stay with her uncle Ahmad. They will take good care of her. You know how much Uncle Ahmad's wife likes her." Mother always hoped Mina would one day marry Morteza, Uncle Ahmad's son.

"Stop gibbering nonsense. Don't try to take advantage of the situation in favor of your family. That fucking Salimeh Khanum with that faggot son of hers! You'd have to marry him off to a husband not to a wife. I am not going to give my daughter away to Ahmad agha and Jezebel Khanum." Father could not resist any opportunity to criticize Morteza, who had let his hair grow down to his neck, wore fashionable attire, and called himself a Hippie. Mina and Mahnaz loved the way he dressed.

Mina was not giving up, "I'm going to starve myself to death if you don't let me go to Tehran." She hoped they would feel more compassionate toward her if they thought she was in danger.

"Shut up. What do you mean that you are not going to eat? You will *run away*? Go wash your mouth before I slap you hard and break all your teeth. I just can't believe this missy is so hard headed now! She wants to go to Tehran! This is what those garbage books and magazines put into your head. I won't allow you to bring those books home anymore. What kind of father would send a girl to the other side of the world alone?"

"I have never seen such a pushy aggressive girl in my whole life!" Mother complained. "I don't know what happened to you. You were such a quiet girl, studying all the time in school. When did you become so disrespectful to your elders?"

Finally, a week before Pahlavi University's entrance exam, Father gave up. "Ok, ok. Don't whine and moan so much. You are suffocating me. You can go to Shiraz with your mother to take the test for Pahlavi University. You can live in Shiraz only on two conditions: if you get accepted in the medical school, and you live in the girls' dorm."

Pahlavi University's test took five hours. The whole five hours Mina sat staring into the air and thought about Tehran. She thought of the Rahahan Square, the honking of the noisy cars the paved streets, the multi-story buildings, and the neon lights above cinemas. She thought of the North and the restaurant on the shore, the woman with sleeveless colorful dress, and the girl who wore sandals with her toenails painted in red. And she dreamed of becoming an engineer and living in Tehran.

The following year, at the entrance exam of the University of Tehran, despite the weakness caused by months of a food strike, Mina, determined and focused, sat for more than four hours and answered all the questions.

• • •

Mr. Shams, the City Council president and the owner of the only newspaper store in Borazjan, was the first to bring the news to Father, by taking the newspaper to his office.

Mina Sha'abani's name shone like a brilliant diamond in the middle page of Kayhan newspaper, among the hundred other students who were accepted to the Mechanical Engineering College of the University of Tehran.

The news spread throughout the town fast.

"Mr. Sha'abani's daughter is going to live in Tehran!"

"What?"

"She has been accepted to the University of Tehran."

"She is going to be an engineer."

"Can a woman be an engineer?"

"God knows! The Judgment Day approaching. If a girl can go to Tehran and live there alone, she can become an engineer too!"

That night Mina took the newspaper to bed with her and did not sleep until dawn.

• • •

Nov. 1972 /Azar 1350

Mina's friend parked her car a few blocks away and they walked toward the building of the Society of Iran and America on Vozara Street. They had come to see "The Teachers," a much-anticipated play everybody kept talking about in the college. Since coming to Tehran a year and half ago, this was the first time Mina attended an event off-campus.

The first year Mina rented Iran Khanum's basement. Iran Khanum and her family were the only people Mina's family knew in Tehran.   She then moved to the girls' dorm.

Mina had many times refused other students' invitation to cultural events - Cincmas, plays, or the Friday morning hikes. However, seeing a play like this was an opportunity that might not come along for a long time, everybody said.

One block away from the building, stood two students from the College of Visual Arts, a student of the College of Engineering, and some others next to a big bronze sculpture in front of the Society. When they got closer and could recognize the shape of the sculpture, Mina was greatly surprised. She stepped forward and touched the figure, then walked back to see the whole thing again. It was a calligraphic metal sculpture, taller than her. A calligraphy of the word *heech*, nothingness, in the shape of a cat's body.

The students looked upset and talked nervously. Mina had seen some of them in the campus cafeterias, or on the sidewalks around the stonewall surrounding the University of Tehran, discussing politics when the entire university or just some colleges were on strike, or when the police and SAVAK had shut down the university.

Since Mina started college, the Engineering College and some others had gone on strike a few times. The students had marched around the campus, shouting slogans against the White Revolution, the Shah, and the lavish ceremony of the 2,500[th] year of the Persian Empire. Each time the police had intervened and detained a large number of students along with some faculty members. SAVAK had accused some students for their involvement in the Siahkal incident. Mina did not know what the Siahkal was, and uncharacteristically, did not want to know. She did not want any involvement in the conflicts between students and the government.

"There is no play tonight," said one of the students from the College of Visual Arts.

"What a pity, we should've come the first night."

"Last night it was sold out hours before it started."

"The SAVAK agents came and took them an hour ago."

"Did they take the actors, too?"

"No. They only took the director, Soltanpour, and the playwright."

"Don't wait around. They are still here. They are watching and securing the area."

"I saw two of them sitting in a car on the corner."

"Bye. I will see you tomorrow at school."

"We are going to have dinner in the Society's restaurant. Are you coming with us?"

Mina's curiosity to see the Society of Iran and America's restaurant and find out about the play overcame her fear of SAVAK.

The restaurant was big and bright, with a colorful countertop, white lacquered tables and wooden chairs; different from any other restaurant Mina had ever seen. A young couple sitting at the back waved, inviting them to their table. Except for Mina, everybody else knew Zary and Parviz.

"Have you come to see *The Teachers*?" asked one of the guys.

"We saw it last night. If you had come last night, you could have seen Soltanpour himself. After the play we all came here and had dinner," said Parviz, who then turned to Mina and continued, "He sat there, just where you're sitting."

"Two of those stupid SAVAKi's sat at the counter and ate hamburgers," Parviz let out a loud laugh. "They did not know what to do with the ketchup the waiter placed in front of them."

Mina did not know what ketchup was either, or what she was supposed to do with it, but still laughed with the others.

Introductions were made. Parviz was a former student of the Engineering College and Zary was a sophomore in the Business School. Short and dark skinned, Parviz was in his early thirties. After his graduation, he had started a small die casting shop in a poor neighborhood in the south of Tehran. With her petite body, delicate face, and big dark brown eyes, Zary seemed in her twenties.

"How was the play?" Mina asked.

"Doesn't the fact that they seized it on the second night say how good it was?" Parviz let out another laugh. He laughed as though he had heard a funny joke. His big mouth with its prominent lips opened wide, and his eyes were wet with tears.

"You and Zary are on the list now!" exclaimed one of the girls.

"Don't worry about us. Our names have been on their list for a long time now. At least once a month one of them comes to Parviz's shop," Zary said as if she enjoyed having her name on the SAVAK list. "They disguise themselves as workers looking for a job or as a customer, to see what is going on there."

Parviz continued from where Zary stopped. "Though it wouldn't surprise me if they added our names to the list one more time to get a promotion!" He let out another laugh.

They ordered a large pizza for dinner. It was the first time Mina was seeing a pizza. She grabbed her knife and fork and started struggling to cut the piece in her plate. She wasn't an expert using them either.

"Put away your utensil. Just use your fingers." Parviz laughed. "Don't be shy; eat it with your hands".

Mina left the knife and fork next to her plate and grabbed the pizza by hand. She felt more comfortable with the group now. Parviz and Zary's easy manners and friendliness impressed her.

Before they got back to their car, Mina and her friend stopped by the sculpture and watched it one more time. What a strange artwork! A sad, curled *heech* sat on the surface of the street like a cat with a hump on its back, its tail coiled around its legs.

• • •

A few days later, while riding a bus home, Mina saw Parviz got on the bus at the second stop. He looked around and came directly toward Mina, muttered a hello, and sat next to her.

"What a coincidence. Do you take this bus often?" Mina said.

"No, not at all. I followed you from the college," Parviz said. "I want to talk to you. But there are always SAVAK officers in front of the Engineering College."

Mina regarded him in confusion.

"Don't get excited! It's out of romantic interest. Zary knows," he was quite serious. "Do you know where Danesh bookstore is? Can you meet me there in two hours?"

Mina nodded. Parviz got out at the next stop.

Mina was at the bookstore exactly in two hours. Parviz stood next to one of the shelves busying himself with a book. As Mina entered, he looked up, returned the book to the shelf, and walked toward the back of the store. He disappeared behind a faded curtain. Mina followed him. Parviz was waiting for her at the end of the back alley. They walked together to a nearby coffee shop. Parviz did not wait to ask her questions.

"You have a provincial accent," Parviz asked. "Where are you from?"

Mina felt insulted and nervously straightened her blouse. "I come from a town in the South, called

Borazjan." She usually told others that she was from Shiraz, a much bigger and more developed city. "I wasn't aware my accent was so *provincial* that it would get your attention."

"I am sorry. I didn't mean to be rude. I just wanted to know about your background, " said Parviz. "I, too, am from a small town close to Siahkal." He stopped talking and scrutinized Mina's face. "You certainly have heard about that village, haven't you?"

"Oh yeah...," she felt embarrassed. She did not know much. "But...well...can you tell me more about it?" Mina finally asked the question that was on her mind for some time. "What is all this talk about Siahkal?"

"Siahkal is a village in the North surrounded by mountains. About a year ago, a group of revolutionary Marxist-Leninist intellectuals decided to start an armed struggle, a guerrilla movement, from there and then move to the cities, just like in Cuba," Parviz continued in a less upbeat voice. "Unfortunately, right after they attacked the town's gendarmerie post, and before they could do much, they were all arrested and put in Evin prison."

Mina visualized the petite body of Zary coming down from a mountain in the North, wearing an army uniform with a machine gun over her shoulder, shooting at the SAVAK officers and the maître d' of the Motel Qoo's restaurant. Remembering Zary's small shoes, Mina could not believe an army boot existed in that size.

"But why had they started that... what did you call it? The guerrilla movement? Why are all these people, especially the students against the regime?" Mina was truly puzzled. Before she started university, it seemed the only people against the Shah and the royal family were the feudal who had lost their farmlands because of the White Revolution.

"Why? Haven't you seen all the corruption and unfair distribution of wealth in Iran? There must be a lot of poor uneducated people in your town, Borazjan. Haven't you noticed?"

Mina recalled Nane-ye Mohamad's family. "Yes...but Tehran and the North are different. People live a much better life here..."

"Have you seen the shanty town of *Halabiabad*, the Tin City? " Parviz asked.

Mina shook her head.

"Then let's meet at Shoosh Square next week, I will take you to Halabiabad from there. Please wear a scarf or chador so people don't take you as a foreign tourist. You should see how some people live in Tehran. Masses of people live in holes made of tin. Those metal dungeons get hotter than my die cast shop in the summer." He opened his mouth to laugh and his white teeth showed.

Parviz then answered her other questions. "Why did the SAVAK stop the play, *The Teachers*?" For the same reason they block and censor books and magazines; the play was about poverty and political repression. Do you know anything about dictatorship?"

Mina listened to him more attentively as she tried to understand why the university students were mostly on strike, and why every so often someone from her class disappeared in the middle of a term and never came back.

In a week, Zary met her in a cafeteria at the corner of

Naderi Street. After they ordered tea and pastry, Mina asked her other questions. What is Imperialism? Why are the students so against America?

"Imperialism is the natural development of capitalism," Zary said. "It is the way a country like America increases its power over the countries like Iran, to exploit their people and their resources."

But they send free milk for students! Yes, and instead they get most of our oil free. Do you know what the purpose of the White Revolution reforms was? A step toward westernization? Yes, it was but the Shah also needed the support of peasants and working class, and support of the Americans for military assistance. Kennedy and his policies supported these reforms to weaken anti-regime's left wing, hence the Soviet Union's influence in the Middle East. Nevertheless, most people doing much better financially than before. Yes, sure, it is better than before, particularly for the Shah's family! It is just a facade. The oil boom has led to a flood of petro-dollars with which the regime directs some development programs. What is happening in Iran is not a real economic development; it is just a dependent bourgeoisie, a Comprador Bourgeoisie. We sell oil under price to the west and buy the montage technology from them over price. The Shah's family and confidants pocket a good percentage in between.

The next time they met, Zary brought her two books, Tolstoy's *War and Peace*, and Flaubert's *Madame Bovary*.

"Oh, I have read both!" Mina exclaimed.

Zary stared at her, "Read them again," she said.

Mina opened the first one and paged through it. On

the third page, she found the real title: "Capital" by Karl Marx. The second book was *The Elementary Principles of Philosophy* by Georges Politzer. Both covers were disguised for safety reasons.

As their mentoring progressed, Zary and Parviz brought her more books, all banned in Iran: *What Should We Do* by Lenin with the cover of Matheson's *The Feather*; Maxim Gorky's *Mother* with the cover of Pearl Buck's *Mother*. *Revolution in the Revolution* by Régis Debray; *Memoir of a Comrade* by Ashraf Dehghani; *Armed Struggle: a Strategy and Tactic* by Ahmadzadeh and Hegel's *Dialectic in Historical Philosophy* all hidden under the covers of popular novels found in the market.

• • •

Mina's main duty was learning; something she enjoyed. Soon, her vocabulary expanded to include words like "bourgeois," "dictatorship," "proletariat," "dialectic," and "revolution." Now she knew why her city, Borazjan, a small hot town with sandy winds, had such a huge prison, a fortress Mina had passed on her way to school for years, which was under the management of the good-mannered Sergeant Pashaee.

The prison was home to a lot of political prisoners, mostly old members of Toudeh Party, the first Communist party of Iran, and the members and followers of the "Organization of Iranian People's Fadai Guerrillas," which emerged after the Siahkal's attack, the turning point in the armed struggle against the Pahlavi regime.

Now Mina could take part in discussions and pass on her knowledge to new students.

Eventually Zary and Parviz stopped showing up on campus. Every time they met, they told her where to see each other the next time; always in a new bookstore or cafeteria, and in a different neighborhood.

On the second year of their friendship, Mina was asked to carry some packages for them. It was a good feeling. They trusted her! She did not get to know the people she carried the bundles to, and she was not allowed to talk about these missions with anybody.

In the middle of March, the University closed for Nowruz holidays. When Mina came back from Borazjan in early April, the school was on strike again. All nine Siahkal famous prisoners had been executed. The government announced that they were shot while attempting to escape the prison. Nobody believed it. The Shah was visiting the US at the time. The rumor was he had the prisoners killed on the recommendation of his American military advisors. He wanted to assure the Americans of the safety of the country, of its being the Island of Stability in the region.

The prisoners had kept active regardless of their captivity. One of them, Bijan Jazany, had led the leftist movement from within the prison. He had even written two books and sent them out of prison. The books were published underground and copies were circulating among intellectuals.

"Can we meet again this week?" Zary told her in their first meeting after the holidays.

"Sure, where do you want to meet?"

"Meet Parviz at Paris Pastry tomorrow at eleven in

the morning," said Zary. "By the way, carry with you two big books in a shopping bag."

Mina was surprised. This was the first time she would meet them two days in a row. Why eleven in the morning? They usually met in the afternoon, after school. What are the books for? Which books should she take with her?

The next morning, Radio Iran had a big announcement. "A car carrying two U.S. Air Force officers was trapped between two cars carrying armed men. The armed men told the Iranian driver to lie down and then shot and killed the Americans." The newscaster added then, "The officers were on their way to work at the military base southeast of Tehran."

At eleven sharp, Mina was at Paris Pastry, carrying two books in a shopping bag. Parviz was not there yet. She sat in a dark corner and ordered coffee. When she finished her coffee, she checked her watch. It was 11:15. She waited fifteen minutes more, then called the waiter and asked him the time. It was 11:30. Parviz was never that late. *Maybe it's too dark here.* She moved to a brighter side of the bakery and ordered another coffee.

She left at 12 sharp. It was an order. She should not wait more than an hour if they did not show up for a meeting. She must leave and not go home directly.

As she stepped out, a man obviously in a rush collided her. Mina fell down and her bag dropped. The man had a hairy mustache and wore a thick eyeglasses.

"I am sorry Miss. I am very sorry." He helped Mina get up, handed her her bag, and left in a hurry.

Mina straightened her hair and dress, and walked away. Something felt odd. She did not know what. Was she dizzy? Had she hurt her arms? The shopping bag seemed strange. She opened it. The two books were still there. She kept walking. The bag felt heavier. She opened the bag again and touched the books. They were not the same books! She touched them again. No, they weren't her books. She withdrew her hand quickly and looked around. No one was watching. She walked faster and left the area quickly.

When she got home she first locked all the doors, then took the books out of the bag. One of them was a box designed to look like a book. She tried to open it but it was locked. What was she supposed to do with it? She put it back and opened the other book. There was nothing special about that one. It was a real book with less than a hundred pages. She put the bag away and went back to school. If she had to do anything, someone would contact her and let her know.

There was a large gathering in front of the University. Police and military surrounded them. They checked any student who wanted to enter. They occasionally arrested people, handcuffed them, and put them on a police car. Mina panicked. Would they arrest her too? She turned back and rushed home.

She waited at the corner for half an hour and checked all the traffic going in and out of her building. She entered her apartment after she had made sure no one was watching her.

• • •

What was she supposed to do now? Where and when should she see Zary or Parviz? She tried to open the box again. No success. She shook it cautiously. Something heavy moved inside. Was it a gun? What was she supposed to do with it, if it were?

She put aside the box and opened the book. Just an ordinary book. It was not even new. Someone had read it before and put notes on several pages. Oh... that's it! There must be a message among the notes.

She spent a few hours reading all the notes carefully. Nothing specific: "What does this mean?" "Not a good narration"; "Bad word choice." All meaningless to Mina. She inspected the box again. Maybe she should find a way to open it. The instruction could be inside the box. It was not easy to open it. Besides, what if there was a gun inside? Possessing a weapon was more dangerous than possessing a box. If someone discovered the box, she could say she did not know what was inside, she had found it when her bag was mixed up with someone else's.

She hid the box among her other books and took the small book to bed with her. She read all the notes again. No clue at all.

She woke up in the middle of the night. If the answer was not in the notes, it must be in the book itself. She jumped out of the bed, grabbed the book and started reading. On page twenty, on the first line one letter was underlined with a very fine point pencil. Another letter on page twenty one and then two on the following pages. She wrote down the letters on a piece of paper. After she finished the book, what she had come up with was: Shademan, the same time, the same day. There was a bookstore on Shademan Ave where Mina had met Parviz before. Great. That was it. They had met at four in the evening on a Thursday. She was supposed to take the box to Shademan Ave. on Thursday at four. Tomorrow was Thursday.

She did not go back to bed. She washed her face and made tea. She was happy. She had decoded the book. They had trusted her with such an important mission.

After she had her second glass of hot tea, she held the book above the burner and when the flames sparked, she put it in the sink. When nothing but a pile of ashes remained of the book, she opened the faucet and washed it out.

Mina put the box in her school bag and left home. The bookstore was on the east side of the city. She could get a taxi but she decided to go by bus. It would take her three buses, but she had lots of time. At the end of the first line, she walked couple of blocks. Before taking the second bus, she looked around. No one was following her. The streets were quiet. She wished she were in the university so that she could join others in protesting the massacre of Siahkal heroes. She was in the second bus when the radio announced; "...police have identified three Marxist guerrillas who stopped the American's car on Wednesday and shot the officers to death..."

Oh...did *they* do it? Have I been part of the scheme? Am I a hero now? But two people have been murdered. No, I am not a murderer. I don't want to be involved in a crime. She clutched her school bag and looked around. She felt people were looking at her furtively. Was anyone of them a SAVAK agent? Her heart started beating hard. She put the bag down, and with the tip of her shoe, she moved it under the seat. Would they send her to the Borazjan prison? What a scandal! Most of the people in

Borazjan knew her now. People respected Mother and Father more because of her. All her prior teachers and classmates were proud that one of them had improved so much. Even Mrs. Tashakori who did not like her before, now bragged about Mina being one of her dear students. She was supposed to be a role model for other girls. If she was arrested or something went wrong, no one would let his or her daughter to go to Tehran to study anymore.

She got off the bus at the next stop and left the bag behind.

She did not hear from Zary or Parviz for many years.

• • •

Right after her graduation, Mina found a job at a major consulting company. Her engineering degree was in great demand. The company worked with foreign firms in carrying out industrial development projects.

She didn't inform her parents about the job for a few months. She was not ready for a new round of battles. She had promised them she would go back right after the graduation. Mahnaz, who lived with her now, was the only relative who knew about her job. For Mahnaz, moving to Tehran was easy. She could stay with Mina. The family was happy; the two sisters could watch out after each other. Hossein had gone to America months ago.

Bahram, Iran Khanum's son was the next to hear about the job. When Mina lived with them, she avoided him as much as possible. Everyone had advised her to be cautious with Tehrani boys. Nevertheless, as the years passed, she and Bahram became closer. Bahram was not the kind to try to take advantage of her. He was virtuous and moral. Bahram now worked as a bank teller.

After Mina moved out of Iran Khanum's house, at first she went to visit them every Friday. Then she did whenever she craved a good home-cooked meal. Iran Khanum's cooking was no less perfect than Mother's. Some of her recipes, though, were different from Mother's, especially Mina's favorite dish, *kalam polo*. Mother used to cook *kalam polo* using kohlrabi, fresh herbs, and meatballs. Iran Khanum, however, used light green-leave cabbages and lamb shank, no herbs added. Mina loved both.

Mina and Bahram usually discussed politics and social issues. He was particularly interested in discussing religion, as he knew Mina was a non-believer.

"The religion you have been introduced to over the years is not the true Islam," said Bahram. "If you listen to researchers of true Islam, people like Dr. Shari'ati, you won't say anything against it."

That was the first time Mina was hearing about Dr. Shari'ati. Bahram continued, "He has a PhD in sociology of religion from the Sorbonne and knows about politics as much as any of your Marxists teachers."

The next time Mina went to Iran Khanum's house, Bahram gave her a book. *Rebirth of Islam: A Quick Look at Over a Century* by Dr. Shari'ati.

"What is this?" She asked.

"This is a good book to read to clear your mind about Islam."

"I don't have time to read it now," said Mina

impatiently. "Tell me about it, I will read it later."

"He talks about Islam not only as a religion of piety and scholarship, but as a system which includes the essential elements of socio-political activism," Bahram said.

Mina put the book aside to read when she got a chance, a chance that would never come. Another book Bahram gave her, *Fatimah is Fatimah*, caught Mina's eyes. He insisted that the book introduced the true ideal for a Muslim woman. She started to read it the same day.

When she finished it, she was greatly dumbfounded. A true ideal for a woman? Bahram must have been teasing her. The book was about the life of Fatimah, the Prophet's daughter, a life full of piety, submission, and sacrifice; her marriage to her father's cousin Ali ibn Abi Talib, the first Imam of the Shiite Muslims, at the age of nine; and her death at the age of eighteen. Poor girl! She gave birth to five kids, including Imam Hossein, at such a young age.

Bahram was serious. He defended anything Shari'ati said with an enthusiasm and excitement that Mina had never seen in him. Bahram spoke as if Imam Hossein was the most revolutionary of all in the world; and the desert of Karbala was the greatest battlefield between truth and falsehood, good and evil, as well as right and wrong; and Lady Zainab, Imam Hossein's sister and defender, was the teacher and mentor of Djamila Bouhired the famous Algerian revolutionary.

The jargon Bahram used was mostly new to Mina, "revolutionary Islam," "martyrdom and imamate," and "religious leadership". Later on, she heard them, time and again, from different people.

When Iran Khanum heard Mina was planning to stay in Tehran, she called Mother and asked her for Mina's hand in marriage for Bahram.

After that, Mina stopped going to their house.

• • •

It was still early in the morning when Mina heard the door buzz. She opened the door. There stood a dark-complexioned, slim man with dark glasses holding a dusty jacket on his hand. He was pale with disheveled greasy hair. His once bushy mustache was shaven.

"Oh my God! It is Parviz! How much you've changed!"

Parviz peeked inside, then walked in. He leaned against a wall and asked Mina to close the curtains. The room darkened. He sat on the far end of the sofa near the door. Mina was in her pajamas, and had not yet washed her face or brushed her teeth. As she made a move to go to the bedroom, Parviz jolted up, "Where are you going?"

"To the bedroom to change!" Mina responded.

"Your dress is ok. Stay in this room," his tone was unfamiliar. "As long as I am here, you will stay in this room. Don't approach the window either."

"Would you like some tea?" Mina asked.

"No."

"Water?"

"No, I don't want anything." He sounded impatient.

Mina followed his gaze towards the telephone. Without him asking, she disconnected the phone, and sat across from him and listened to his story.

Parviz had lived in a safe house with some comrades after the shooting of the American colonels. None of them were involved in the assassination; nevertheless, they all had to go to hideouts. SAVAK had started a vigilant search and brutal torture of political prisoners to find anyone connected with the case. A year before, he had spotted SAVAK agents outside his hideout, - three men with dark glasses - in a black Ford, waiting for him at the end of the street, while two others waited at the other side of the street in a white Mercedes. Since then he had not had a place to stay. He had lived with a friend or an acquaintance for a short while and then moved on to the next place. He walked the streets for many days and nights and went without food for many days and nights. He had not seen Zary ever since he went into hiding.

"Is there anything I can do?" Mina asked.

"Do you have any cash at home?"

The day before she had changed the last hundred toman bill left from her last paycheck.

"I don't have much cash in my wallet. But I always keep some cash in my various handbags for rainy days," she looked at Parviz. "Can I go look for them?"

Parviz stared at her suspiciously.

"We can search together." Mina retorted irritably.

"Please forgive me. I have to be cautious. These sons of bitches can do anything. They have interrogated some of my friends and family members," Parviz's voice broke. "Zary has been under brutal torture In the prison for a year now."

They went without talking for a minute. "How long did they gave her?" asked Mina.

"Nobody knows. If she survives the tortures, they might keep her there forever."

"Don't worry," said Mina softly. "They haven't come to me yet."

Parviz apologized and gestured that she could go.

Mina found a one-hundred-toman bill, two fifty-tomans, and twenty seven singles, the remains of yesterday's shopping. Parviz took the money in silence and got up to leave. Mina accompanied him.

Before he opens the door, Mina removed her necklace and handed it to him, "What about this? It might be of use."

The necklace was an antique pendant Mother had given her to protect her from the evil eyes, on a gold chain. Engraved on the pendant was a Quran verse: "those who disbelieve would almost smite you with their eyes."

Parviz gazed at her while Mina hung the gold chain around his neck. Mina burst into sobs. Parviz pressed her head to his bony chest and stroked her hair while she cried.

• • •

<u>Oct. 1977 / Aban 1356</u>

It was the third night of the Ten Nights of Poetry Reading held in the summer garden of the Goethe Institute. In the previous years, poetry readings had regularly been held at the cultural society of Iran and Germany in the north part of Tehran, but this was the first year the Iranian Writers' Association, which, because of their anti-government position, had been banned from any activity for years, had partnered with them. When Mina and Mahnaz got there, the gate was closed and a group of disappointed people was knocking at it. The garden had filled up two hours ago.

A tall dark-haired man wearing a pair of thick eyeglasses opened the gate. The outcry stopped. Some whispered, Dr. Khoei.

"He is a poet, a revolutionary poet," Mahnaz mumbled under Mina's ear. "He has many poems against the Shah's corrupt regime."

After exchanging some words with the crowd, the poet hesitantly moved away from the gate. People pushed the gate. The door opened slowly and before a guard closed it, some people, including Mina and Mahnaz, rushed in.

Mina saw some of her college classmates among the audience and nodded a hello to them. many people carried posters and placards inscribed with poetry. Mina only recognized Forough Farrokhzad's "Remember the Flight / the bird is mortal."

Unlike Mina, Mahnaz had loved poems since she was a child. In school, her books were recognizable from other students' because she wrote a Sa'di's *ghazal* on them. The mysticism of classical poetry, which Father and Mahnaz loved, was not appealing to Mina, and she did not grasp modern poetry well.

On the fifth night, Mina enthusiastically attended the poetry reading again. That night Saeed Soltanpour was to recite his poems. If Mina had failed to see his play, at least she should hear him recite his poetry.

Mina arrived two hours ahead of the schedule, but

the garden was full again. With the help of others, Mina climbed and sat on top of a wall. When Soltanpour arrived, a loud cheer rose from the crowd. He raised his hand and invited people to calm down.

"Welcome. Welcome you broken people of the dark years, thirsty for freedom. My sisters and brothers, I salute you! As a member of the Iranian Writers Association, holding on to the independence of my thoughts and accepting full responsibility for my beliefs, I speak to you of the Association and recite poems ..."

Prolonged applause interrupted him. He smiled humbly and read from his poetry:

What has happened to my country,
What has happened to my home,
That the prisons are filled with tulips and dews.

The crowd interrupted him several times and gave him standing ovations. His poetry was the language of resistance and revolt.

Mina attended the remaining five nights, though the last two nights she had to stand in the alley behind the closed gate to listen to the poets' voices.

On the final night, after listening to the concluding announcement of the event, Mina walked part of the route to her house with Mahnaz and others. Along the way, they shouted several times, "What has happened to my country, what has happened to my home, that the prisons are filled with tulips and dews," and discussed the words "tulip" and "dew" and their connoting political prisoners.

Mina now appreciated the use of the metaphors like 'blood,' 'crimson dawn,' and 'dark winter,' which were often used in modern poetry. She had become a bird desiring flight.

• • •

A few weeks later, Mina saw a group of people listening to Dr. Shari'ati's speech through loud-speakers in front of a building close to her office.

"... Religion is the path to life, salvation, and perfection of human beings. Religion is the answer to the deepest and highest human needs. Therefore..."

Except for a large green neon sign that read *Allah o Akbar*, the building did not resemble a mosque.

Bahram was right in one aspect; Dr. Shari'ati's preaching did not resemble other preachers'.

For as far back as Mina could remember, on the evening of the first Thursday of each month, Mullah Hassan, the neighborhood's mullah, came to their house and gave a sermon on Imam Hossein and the events of Karbala, of Lady Zainab, and the martyrdom of the two innocent Sons of Moslem. Mother put on an old black chador, sat with Nane-ye Mohammad at the other end of the room, and they both wept for the massacre of the Imam and his family. Even when Mother was not home, Mina or Mahnaz led Mullah Hassan to the guestroom; he recited the passions, and then left. Mother always put a five-toman bill on the shelf and Mullah Hassan pocketed it once he was done with his recitation.

The next day she called Bahram's house to talk to him. He was not home. Iran Khanum invited her for the next Friday's lunch. It was about a year since she had seen any of them. She accepted Iran Khanum's

73

invitation. She longed for a nice homemade dish like the ones Mother cooked.

● ● ●

While getting ready to go to Iran Khanum's, Mina heard the news on the radio. She turned the radio on as soon as she sat in her new Paykan, the car she had recently bought with a loan from her work. The government announced the execution of martial law starting that night. Nobody should be out from 7.00 pm until 6.00 am the following day.

It could be a good excuse not to spend much time with them, she thought.

There was another broadcast while driving to Rahahan Square. She turned the volume up: "According to our reports, there has been a violent clash between the police forces and a group of people gathered in Jaleh Square this morning. The number of casualties is not clear yet."

Iran Khanum, distressed and anxious, waited for her at the door.

"Bahram and Azar went to Jaleh Square this morning to protest the curfew," she said. "I have to go find them." Mina went along with her.

Jaleh Square was at least an hour away. With too many people heading in the same direction, the traffic became heavier as they got closer. It came to a complete halt not far from the Square. The stalled cars began honking their horns to show their frustration. A black thick column of smoke was visible from afar. Two khaki military helicopters flew over. The sound of gunfire mixed with the voices of people chanting *Allah o Akbar*.

Every time she heard the chanting, Iran Khanum wept harder and scratched her face with her fingernails. Suddenly, she opened the door, jumped out, and began walking. Mina left the car running and ran after her. She took her by the arm and forced her back into the car. She then asked other drivers to move their cars and pulled over to the side. Mina double-parked the car, made Iran Khanum promise to stay in the car, and headed toward the Square.

Armed forces surrounded Jaleh Square, and the Royal Guards took position behind military vehicles and tanks. A young soldier, holding an automatic rifle, sat on top of a tank. He was so young that his mustache had not fully grown yet.

"May I go this way?" pleaded Mina. "My brother came to Jaleh Square this morning and he hasn't returned yet."

The guard aimed his rifle at her. "Go away before I shoot you."

Mina changed her direction. Three blocks further, she joined a group of people trying to find a way through. She doubted she could find Bahram and Azar in that crowd, but she needed to know what was going on. Who were these people? Why had Bahram risked his life to be here?

She heard a loud explosion and turned toward the direction of the blast. A blanket of white smoke covered the area. It was a tear gas. Tears streamed down her face. The crowd scattered and fled in all directions. Mina ran aimlessly. After a few minutes, she turned into a narrow alley and stopped.

She felt nauseated and started vomiting until there was nothing left in her stomach. She wiped her eyes and looked around. Now she could see clearly. On the other side of the alley, a girl leaned against the wall, one of her legs stretched out in front of her. A narrow stream of blood ran from the side of her belly and continued by her foot. She held her wound with both hands. Mina ran toward her. "Miss, Miss, Are you okay?" "Miss, do you need help?"

The girl opened and closed her eyes. Her pants were blood-soaked. The bullet had passed through the flesh. Using her teeth, Mina tore the corner of the girl's long loose blouse and tied it firmly around her waist. The bleeding slowed down after a few seconds.

The girl was awfully pale, as if there was no blood left in her body. What could Mina do for her? How could she get her to the car? She thought about getting help from someone. She rushed to one of the houses, but before she got there, the girl let out one last moan and grew silent. Mina turned and looked at her. She was dead.

• • •

Religious leaders had invited everyone to attend a rally on the festive day of *Eid-al-Fitr*. At the office, Mina's colleagues discussed the issue. Should they participate? The army had attacked the previous rallies and killed some people. Mina could not forget the dead girl in the alley. What was going on? Was it safe to go? Would the SAVAK single them out?

Eventually Mina and her colleagues decided to join

others. The crowd marched from north of Tehran toward Shahyaad Square in the southwest. Mina stood aside in the sidewalk, watching the protesters.

The silence of the Muslims is a betrayal of the Quran,
The silence of the Muslims is a betrayal of the Quran.

Among the crowd were women and men in suits, student boys and girls in jeans, mullahs wearing turbans, as well as women in chadors. Mina was more than anything surprised at seeing so many women covered in black chadors. Who were these women? For sure, they were not Shari'ati's followers. They looked more traditional, like simple religious women she had seen in the streets and the mosques. The slogans were new to Mina:

Imam Hossein our protector,
Khomeini our leader.
Khomeini must return,
Khomeini must return,

Although the military forces were not present, the protesters, every now and then shouted: "Oh, army brother, why do you kill your brothers?"

Mina watched the marching crowd for two hours without joining them. What was going on? Wasn't religion the opium of the masses?

• • •

Mina woke up to the shouts of *Allah o Akbar* and the sound of gunfire. It was shortly after midnight. She got up and went to the window. Nobody was in the street. The voices came from the rooftops.

The next night, Mina saw two people coming out of a house, both wrapped in a white shroud from head to toe. They passed the street and disappeared on the other side. An hour later, she saw a few people covering their faces with masks and carrying guns, walking cautiously to a parked car, jumping in and taking off immediately. Mina went back to bed but could not sleep.

Recently she had received another letter from Hossein. He sounded happy, but not in college yet. Still learning English and having fun with girls. He sent a picture of him next to a blond girl in a bikini at a beach. It seemed like a different planet. She wanted to go visit him or move there to study. But what about all these happenings? She needed to stay and witness the changes, fight for everything Parviz, Zary, and all the books she had read had promoted all these years, for all the ideas she had grown to believe in.

In the morning, Mina arrived at work late. Her co-workers were engaged in a debate, as they were all month long. The subject of the talk was the public announcement of another rally for the Shia's mourning day of *Tasu'a* by both religious groups and a coalition of Mosaddegh's followers called Jebhe Meli, the National front.

Before Mina left the office, Zary called "Please meet me and other people from our group tomorrow at Peech-e Shemiran, at 7:00." She had been freed from prison along with many others, when a group of students had opened the gates of Evin Prison a few weeks earlier. "We will have our own group, but walk along demonstrators not to be singled out by SAVAK."

• • •

A large number of women were among the participants, mostly in black chadors or headscarves or both. Two women wearing chadors and masks held the two ends of a banner as wide as the street.

"Independence, Freedom, Islamic Republic"

Mina saw a group of young people in a corner, girls all dressed just like her, a pair of jeans with a long tunic and sneakers. Zary was not among them. She walked faster along the crowd in case Zary was ahead of her. After half an hour, she gave up and joined the crowd.

Soon, an elderly woman pulled a black headscarf out of her handbag and offered it to Mina. *A headscarf?* No, thanks! I do not wear a headscarf. She had not worn a scarf since she had left Borazjan.

A military helicopter flew over the throng of people. At times, it hovered over them very low, then twirled around and flew away only to reappear moments later. Two young women in black chador walked on each side of Mina. One of them held a toddler's hand, a boy of two or three years. As he got tired, his mother picked him up and carried him in her arms. Very soon, the boy fell asleep and rested his head on his mother's shoulder. The woman on the other side held a grumpy infant in her arms while her husband held the hand of their seven-year-old daughter, the girl enveloped in a short black chador, the two sides of her chador pinned under her chin, leaving only her plump round face visible. Her dark brown curious eyes wandered around in all directions and her tightly pressed lips gave the impression that she was about to cry. She held a placard of Ayatollah Khomeini's image in her hand. He sat cross-legged leaning backward on the floor, gazing into the distance. This must have been taken in Paris, Mina thought.

The crowd chanted slogans inscribed on banners carried by a number of protesters:

Independence, Freedom, Islamic Republic!
Independence, Freedom, Islamic Republic!

One kilometer down, right before they approached the University of Tehran, another group of protesters joined them. Was this Zary's group?

The group looked shy of the main demonstrators and did not chant their slogans. A number of them carried small banners: "Long Live Democracy, Long Live Freedom" ,"Death to the Shah, Death to the Shah" , "Bread, Housing, Freedom"

The women of the group, the majority of them young, wore no chador or scarf, only simple tunics and trousers, mostly jeans or khakis.

Maybe she should join them. They looked more like her peers. Mina now carried the toddler boy in her arms. She looked at the boy's mother; she was carrying the other woman's grumpy infant.

In front of the University of Tehran, a young security guard approached Mina, She wore a black chador over her headscarf.

"Please put this on," the woman said while presenting a black headscarf to Mina.

Mina looked at her with hesitation. "Just in respect to others," the security guard said. Mina looked over her shoulder to see if the non-religious group was still in view. They were far behind.

Mina returned the boy to his mother and reluctantly put the scarf on.

It took them three hours to get to the Shahyaad Square. In the center of the square, a middle-aged unshaved man stood on top of the Shahyaad Tower, which was built a year after Mina moved to Tehran, on the commemoration of the 2,500[th] anniversary of the Persian Empire. The man read the protestors' manifesto over a loudspeaker while people poured into the square. The manifesto affirmed Khomeini's leadership, called for the abolishment of the monarchy, and demanded social justice. The crowd cheered after each segment.

Leaving the crowd, Mina kissed the other women good-bye, although until only a few hours earlier they had been total strangers.

She was completely exhausted when she got home. Had she really walked six kilometers with one million demonstrators chanting for the establishment of an Islamic state?

So many people on the streets. How unusual! All simple men and women, mostly workers from the lower middle class. All against the regime. But what if they were the ones who sat a cinema on fire and killed many people, only because it was showing obscene movies? How about Ayatollah Khomeini's disapproval of the women's rights?

But the masses were his followers. They did everything he said. What would Parviz have done if he were in her situation? How many people could they, the communists, inspire to go to the streets and march against the regime? The workers had mistrusted them when they went to their neighborhoods to educate them. One of them even threatened Mina to inform the SAVAK if she talked any more about poverty and their miserable lives. Now she wasn't afraid of the SAVAK anymore.

Could they, the leftists, fight SAVAK? It was hard to believe the CIA would let the communists defeat the Shah.

Tehran - Revolution

Jan. 16th, 1979 /26 Day 1357

The announcement was shocking: "Today at 1:00 pm, the Shah and Shahbanoo, escorted by state officials and dignitaries, including the Prime Minister Shahpoor Bakhtiyar, departed the country from Mehrabad Airport. In a brief announcement to reporters, Shahanshah, the King-of-kings, said they were leaving Tehran for a short vacation in Aswan, Egypt."

Everyone in the office, jumped up and down and congratulated each other. Mina threw her arms around Ms. Mehrabi's shoulder and they kissed each other. Here it went Pahlavi's dynasty! What happened to all those shouts of "Long live Pahlavi's dynasty"?

They shut the office three hours before the normal closing time, and mostly went toward the University of Tehran.

A group of dancing people approached them on the way, "Please sweet your mouth," said a woman, all covered in a chador, offering them a box of chocolate.

"Honk! Don't forget to honk!" shouted a slick old man, standing on the sidewalk.

Mina got off the car and walked to the 24 of Esfand Square near the university. She was too anxious to wait.

The sound of the horns was deafening. Pictures of the Shah burned in flames everywhere. There he was dressed in a military uniform, in a black tuxedo, in a pilot gear flying a helicopter, or in casual attire sitting next to his family at his summer palace in the North. His piercing eyes and sharp steadfast gaze were the last parts of him turning into ashes. It was a long time since the University had been free of armed vehicles and Imperial Guards.

Before she went home, more news was broadcasted: Ayatollah Khomeini would return to Iran in a few weeks.

• • •

Feb. 1st, 1979 / 12 Bahman 1357

Mina stayed home that Friday. She wanted to watch the arrival of Ayatollah Khomeini on TV. She stated with the weekly cleanup very early. She swept the entire apartment; then dusted the bookshelves, the dining table, the chairs, and the television. She didn't clean the windows as she usually did. She was in a hurry to finish the cleaning before the TV program started. Although they did not announce it, Mina was sure the TV would show at least part of the event. Khomeini had many supporters among the national TV employees.

Although Mina went to office the other days of the week, she did not really work. No one did. They had tea, discussed politics, and then left to attend a political lecture, a funeral, to visit the bookstores, or go to the University of Tehran to buy or glance at the formerly banned newly published books offered by street vendors on the curbsides. They mostly returned in the afternoon to discuss whatever the day's hot subjects were.

The television showed its usual Friday morning program, Sesame Street. At ten, the screen darkened and stayed dark while someone announced, "Dear audience! In a few moments you will be shown the formal procedure of Ayatollah Khomeini's arrival in Tehran." Mina left the potatoes she was peeling in the bowl to give all her attention to the TV.

The camera showed the inside of a plane for a few minutes, then moved to Khomeini's face. His head bent down, he played with his long gray beard with one hand and counted his rosary with the other. One reporter, whose face could not be seen, asked him in English: "Now that you are back in Iran after fifteen years, how do you feel?" Someone translated the question. Without lifting his head, Ayatollah Khomeini said, ""Nothing." Suddenly Sesame Street returned to the screen.

Mina waited for half an hour, then turned up the volume and went to take a shower. She left the door open just in case there were more news. What did he mean by "Nothing?" He really had no feelings coming back home after all those years?

Mina was blow-drying her hair when the TV turned silent. She went back to the living room. It was showing an Air France plane landing in Mehrabad Airport. After a short while, Khomeini appeared on the top of the stairs. The crowd chanted loudly:

Allah o Akbar!
Allah o Akbar !

The Ayatollah waved at the people gathering at the foot of the plane. His eyes, sheltered under his bushy eyebrows, concealing his emotions. His long beard was neatly shaped and beautiful. He lowered his head and slowly descended the stairs. Mina fixed her eyes on him; she felt possessed by his spirit. As Khomeini's foot touched the ground, tears streamed down her face. The camera turned to the chanting mass:

We are all your soldiers, Khomeini
We are all your soldiers, Khomeini

She could not sit still. She watched TV standing up while indifferently taking the rollers out of her hair and dropping them next to the dryer in the middle of the room. Suddenly, the crowd disappeared and the Shah's image showed on the screen. It was an old picture of him, a smiling young Shah, returning to Tehran years ago after the CIA-backed 1953 coup d'état. Astonished, Mina waited to see more of Khomeini's arrival, but the silent picture of the Shah remained. Were they reminding people of the coup? Mina turned on the radio. It didn't have any announcement either.

"Bastards, they blocked the program!" Mina shouted angrily.

She held her hair back with a narrow, brown elastic band, put on a pair of baggy jeans and a light jacket - the first things she found - and left home. No need to take her car; she could get a ride with people who were on their way to see the Ayatollah's arrival.

A ragged old Hillman stopped next to her. "Are you going anywhere in Ayatollah Khomeini's direction?" she asked. The driver, a clean-cut and clean-shaven young man, and his wife, his two daughters, and his son, excitedly and simultaneously told her they were going to see Imam's arrival, but they did not know how to get there. They hoped she knew.

It had been announced that upon his arrival, Ayatollah would go to Tehran's Behesht e Zahra cemetery, to visit and pay respect to the martyrs of the Revolution. Mina thought Hassanabad Square would be the best place to catch up with his motorcade.

The man parked the car several blocks away from the square. It was faster to walk there. Mina forced her way through the masses of people gathered on the sidewalks. As Khomeini's red and green American GMC approached, she saw a group of men running around the car trying to reach it, as if a sacred moving monument. Three other men sitting on the roof of the car yelled at the running group. Khomeini sat alone in the back seat, his head lowered, seemingly oblivious to the attention of the crowd. People on both sides of the street shouted with joy:

We are your soldiers, Khomeini!

Khomeini raised his head, looked at the swarm of people and waved to them for a short while, then lowered it emotionlessly. Was he still untouched by all that was going on around him?

As his procession disappeared, Mina stood there puzzled. She had never been religious or even spiritual, then why was *she* so preoccupied with him? As she started walking, she felt the spell fading, but still wondering, how could she be so haunted by a person who wasn't even touched with the emotion of millions? Who was this man?

Upon his arrival to the cemetery, Khomeini appointed Mr. Bazargan as the interim prime minister while Shah's last prime minster, Bakhtiar, was still in power. Now the country had two governments.

• • •

Feb. 8 1979 / Bahman 19, 1357

Two young women were holding the ends of a banner that read:

Commemorating 19th of Bahman, the anniversary of Siahkal Epic.

They walked in front of a long line of people stretched from one side of the University of Tehran's campus, to the other.

The number of people showing up for the event was more than what Mina expected. Zary was among the security guards. Unlike other guards, she had not concealed her face with a mask. She stood next to a man who had covered his head and a part of his face with a black-and-white Palestinian Keffiyeh. Zary waved to Mina and then whispered something to the man. Was he Parviz? No, Parviz was much shorter.

Mina stood next to a group of young students she

had met at another rally supporting Prime Minister Bazargan. Two boys held a large red banner. "Salute to the martyrs of Siahkal."

The crowd began to move after an hour. Before getting to the gate, Mina saw Zary and the man in Kaffiyeh again. Zary introduced them to each other, "Comrade Mohsen."

Mina saw nothing more than the man's big, curious eyes and thick eyebrows. "Nice meeting you. Zary said good things about you," he scrutinized Mina's face. The lein moved forward and they didn't get to say anything to each other more than "See you soon."

The demonstrators walked onto Shah-Reza Avenue and toward Shahyaad Square, which people had begun to call Azadi, the freedom, Square now.

The marchers had not completely left the campus when they came to a halt. The security guards had ordered them to stop. Mina took the opportunity to get to know a few people around her. Some young men wore jeans and t-shirts bearing a picture of Che Guevara in a beret with a red-star pin. A group of students had a heated debate about the legitimacy of Bazargan's new government.

"Didn't he accept the Shah as the legitimate head of state?" asked one of the young people.

"But he also was jailed by the Shah's regime for his political activities."

"Don't forget that he was the first head of the Iran's National Oil Company appointed by Mosaddegh," Mina said.

"He is an academic who believes in liberal-democratic Islamic thought. This is what we might need, a transitional government. We need someone like him," said another person. Mina nodded in agreement.

The line started moving; it was directed to move toward the eastern entrance to the university. Soon the news circulated: The flight technicians in Dooshan-Tappeh Air Base had revolted against their officers. It was highly possible that the army would attack them.

Ten minutes later, the line stopped again. The loudspeakers ordered, "if possible, please rush to the Air Force Base in Doshan Tepeh to help the personnel who are on strike."

Mohsen, riding a motorcycle, stopped next to Zary. Zary jumped on the back of the motorcycle and held him tightly. Mohsen zigzagged through the crowd and swiftly went toward the air base.

• • •

Feb. 10-11, 1979 / Bahman 21-22, 1357

A young mullah stood at the back of a fast-moving truck and held a banner. "Stay in the streets. Imam commanded not to go home tonight." His cloak was flowing in the wind.

News circulated by word of mouth. The night before in some military bases, fights had broken out between the Shah's supporters and Khomeini's. Ordinary people alongside the armed Fadai and Mujahedin guerrillas had gone to the air force bases to help the rebels. The government moved the curfew from 7:00 to 4:00 pm. Mina had left the office before three.

She saw a second truck when she was about to turn

onto her street. "Don't go home. There is a conspiracy happening."

The Army wanted to attack the air force camps and kill Bazargan's supporters. Tehran's eastern side had completely become a battlefield. The noise from the shootings and hand grenades came from afar. Military helicopters flew over the streets.

Mina's neighbors were gathering a few blocks down her apartment. She slowed down. "I'll change and be back immediately," she said and rushed home.

"Can you get a container of burned oil from Akbar Agha on your way back?" asked Farhad the Mujahed.

"We have the other materials to make Molotov cocktails."

Mina had seen Farhad two weeks ago while he was spraying on a wall, "Long live People's Mujahedin Organization." She had learned recently that the People's Mujahedin Organization, an Islamic armed group, had branched from a Marxist group, and now followed Dr. Shari'ati's teachings.

Mina lived in an apartment in a four-story building in the middle of the city. One of her colleagues lived with his Belgian wife and his two daughters on the first floor. A dentist and his wife lived in the second floor until a month ago. Following the Shah's departure, the dentist's family put their furniture up for sale and immediately left for England. Mina didn't know the fourth floor neighbors. On the third floor, there were two one-bedroom apartments. Mina had rented the smaller one and two young nurses, had taken the larger one. The nurses usually came back from work in the morning when Mina was leaving for work.

In the corner of the yard, behind the garages, there was a small room where Gholam, the janitor, lived with his wife, two small children, his mother, and his young sister. They stayed in the room for free in exchange for cleaning the building on Fridays. The rest of the week Gholam worked in a nearby bank as a guard and his wife cleaned the neighbors' houses.

Before coming to Tehran, they had a small cotton farm, which they had acquired through *Enghelab e Sefid* reforms, but they had gone bankrupt not too long after.

Mina parked in front of the house, ran in, and changed her clothes. She put on a pair of comfortable jeans, a turtleneck sweater, her sneakers, and grabbed a thick jacket and her transistor radio.

When she got back to the group, black smoke already filled the air. They had set two tires on fire and rolled them into the middle of the street. Mina passed the burned oil to Farhad who had covered half of his face with a cloth.

It did not take Mina long to learn how to make Molotov cocktails. Homa Khanum, a middle-aged teacher, Farhad the Mojahed, and Mina made the cocktails and passed them to Hassan, a soldier who had ran away from the Bagheshah military base a few days ago, and other people. Both Hassan and Farhad were armed.

Hassan threw the first Molotov cocktail. Farhad hurled the second one, and Gholam the third one. Oosta Rajab, the neighborhood's shoemaker, helped Gholam.

One of the cocktails hit the side of a military bus and exploded with a frightening sound. The bus swerved and stopped with a screeching noise. A group of soldiers jumped out, their hands raised above their heads while still holding on to their rifles, and ran away from the bus. Farhad, Oosta Rajab and Hassan ran after them. Two of the soldiers who carried machine guns left them in the middle of the street and disappeared into the darkness of a side street. The rest stopped running and put their weapons down. Farhad and Hassan each picked up one of the machine guns. Oosta Rajab took one of the guns for himself and distributed the rest between others. Mina got one too.

Hassan and Farhad hung the machine guns from their shoulders. Mina thought the machine guns must be part of the artilleries United State had sold to the Shah. She felt an urge to touch them. She went closer and touched the one that Farhad carried. It was cold and smooth.

"Do you want to hold it for a moment?" Farhad picked the machine gun from his shoulder and held it out to Mina.

"No, thanks," she overcame her hesitation. "I just wanted to see how it feels to touch."

The bus was burning in the middle of the street. Fire and smoke rose to the sky. Oosta Rajab and Hassan searched the soldiers and took their bullets and helmets, then let them go. Oosta Rajab put one of the soldier's metal helmets on his head. The gun in hand, helmet on head, wearing a threadbare coat with a cartridge clip hanging over his shoulder, his face gained some gravity.

It was completely dark when Mina saw her next-door neighbor, one of the nurses, joined them. She carried a large bag of first aid supplies. She said she was going to the busier neighborhoods, on foot, to help people in need. She had written her name and phone number on her forearm in case she was killed and someone needed to inform her family.

People started to scatter around 5 am. Mina took two of the bullets and handed the rifle to Oosta Rajab. She kept the bullets in her pocket and played with them all the way home. How could such a soft delicate object become so fatal? She might have killed someone tonight. She had helped to make cocktail Molotov to throw at the soldiers; she had helped to kill men. How easy it was to become a killer.

The light in the nurses' apartment was on. They must have come back safe.

• • •

Zary called the next afternoon. She was crying. "Parviz is martyred. They tortured him to death, the bastards!" her crying faded into a quiet sobbing after a while. Mina listened and wept silently.

One of Zary's friends had found Parviz's name in the documents in a newly discovered secret interrogation house. All types of torture instruments were found at the house: Apollo torture instruments, beam-scale handcuffs, a bed smeared with blood, leather whips. Zary had seen a picture of a tortured, half-burnt body, written above it this words: Parviz Sadri, member of one of the disloyal, anti-people and anti-government subgroups.

Mina wondered how long Parviz had managed to keep hiding safely after visiting her. The Mother's good charm pendant definitely had not kept him safe. Had he at least been able to sell it and use the money?

• • •

March 8, 1979 / Esfand 19, 1357

Rojika, the librarian, arrived a bit late. She looked ridiculous, her hair hidden under a heavy brown scarf tied under her chin.

"Last night Imam Khomeini said women should wear hijab at workplaces," she said shyly, with her thick Armenian accent.

Mina had heard the news the night before, but she didn't take it seriously. She never thought she would be forced to wear hijab. Khomeini had not mentioned mandatory hijab before. It was supposed to be a matter of choice. In his words women were to have equal rights with men:

> *Islam grants woman a say in all affairs, just as it grants man a say... Women enjoy a dignified position; they have free will, just as men have. God created you free beings and gave you dignity... Islam took women by the hand and made them equal with men.*

All the women at the office were angry. They held the first meeting of the Women Committee.

"Today coincides with March 8th, the International Women's Day," said Ms. Mehrabi.

"Two groups of women's rights supporters have invited everyone to celebrate this day at the University. There must be lots of people feeling the same as we do."

"What celebration? We should mourn!"

"We should rally against them," said another woman.

"Protest against whom? Against a revolutionary government? Do you really think this is a right thing to do? Who do you think would take advantage of such rallies?"

"Imperialists and those who deny God!"

"Are you saying we should remain silent and do nothing?"

"You're making rushed conclusions. Imam Khomeini had only mentioned in an interview that it was better if women wear Islamic hijab," said Mr. Akbari, the head of the civil engineering department. "It could be only an advice."

The gathering became chaotic. Everybody talked at the same time in agitated voices. Finally, the majority voted to go to the University and join the March 8th gathering.

Except for Rojika and Yafah, all women left for the rally. Yafah had a good excuse. "I am Jewish. They could fire me right away," she said frankly.

A big crowd, mostly young female employees and students, had gathered in front of the University. No woman wore hijab. Two girls held a big banner.

"In the spring of freedom, freedom is missing"

Around 11:30, the demonstrators moved from the University towards the office of Prime Minister Bazargon. The number of protestors increased, as they got closer. There were many people in the middle of street and on the sidewalks. Contrary to the crowd on the sidewalks, only a few men were in the middle to walk with the protestors. The crowd in the street carried placards made out of cardboard and long wooden handles. "Freedom and equality are our rights. No one can deny it" , "The International Women's Day is neither Western, nor Eastern"

People on the sidewalks held signs too. "The best ornament for women is hijab", "A woman's hijab is dignity of her husband", "A woman with no hijab = a husband with no honor."

"Poor men, our husbands have all lost their honors now," said one of the girls. Everyone laughed. If Maryam Aliabadi were there, she would make everybody laugh all the way, thought Mina. Mina had not seen Maryam for a long time. Maryam now was a housewife and had two sons. She never had time to hang out with Mina when Mina went to Borazjan. They didn't have anything in common anymore.

The people on the sidewalks remained silent while the women in the street protested and cried out their slogans. As they approached the Prime Minister's office, the number of people on the sidewalks increased and they began to shout at the protestors.

A light snow started falling. Mina had on a long overcoat and high boots. Some people had gloves and umbrellas as well. She covered her head with a woolen scarf Mother had knitted for her.

In no time, a layer of snow covered the heads and shoulders of the crowd as well as the dried branches of the bare trees lining the street. Mina had not seen those trees so beautiful before. The snow did not stay on the ground long; it melted under the steps of angry

97

protestors. Ms. Mehrabi and Firouzeh, the receptionist, walked side by side with Mina. The three raised their fists and repeated the slogans shouted by the people in the front line.

Freedom is grace, staying home is disgrace.
Freedom and equality are our undeniable rights.

Ms. Mehrabi suddenly covered her left eye with her hand and shouted in surprise and anger, "Ouch, my eye."

A few women in the back and front rows cried at the same time. A snowball hit Mina's back, and some fell to the ground beside her. A group of young men standing on the sidewalk was responsible. The crowd roared furiously in a louder voice, "Freedom and equality are our unquestionable rights!"

A woman in front of Mina raised her placard. The other women, shaking their fists toward the sidewalks, cried vehemently, "We won't remain in chain."

The snow kept falling. Soon, the street got fully wet. Mina was soaked from head to toe. Drops of water ran down her hair and streamed to her shoulders. All of a sudden, she felt a piercing pain in her face. Her body trembled as if she had been shocked with high voltage electricity. Blood started to spurt from her forehead. A small, sharp stone lay in front of her foot. Everything looked hazy.

"Ladies and gentlemen, please scatter," a voice called through a loudspeaker. "Please disperse. A mob of thugs are throwing stones at the demonstrators."

"Don't go home... come in small groups... in front of the national TV building... we'll continue..." These were the last words Mina heard before she fainted.

Few hours later, she woke up in a hospital bed with a big headache and seven stitches above her eyebrow. She was lucky the stone hit her forehead; Ms. Mehrabi lost sight in one of her eyes and could not return to work for months.

• • •

Two months later, Mina met Mohsen again. Now that his face and head were not covered, Mina could see his receding hairline. Tall and yet somewhat chubby, he appeared to be in his forties. He did not look like a guerrilla at all - at least not the way Mina expected him to be; athletic, muscular, and energetic.

Zary introduced him as one of the heads of the Organization of Iranian People's Fadai Guerrillas (OIPFG).

Mohsen gave Mina her first mission at their first meeting.

"Take this flyer to your office, make copies and distribute them among your co-workers," he smiled. "Make sure the Hezbollah don't see you. The honeymoon is over. They have started making lists of the leftists."

He also asked if he could use her home for political meetings. "I cannot give you any set schedules. When we need it I will inform you through Zary."

Whenever Zary notified her, Mina would hide the key in a place they had agreed on, go to one of her friends', and not return until late at night.

Later on, Mohsen began to come to Mina's home

without prior notice. He examined the home from the outside until he was sure the house was not being watched. He then buzzed the doorbell. One short ring, silence, another short ring. If she were alone, she would open the door. Sometimes he would give her a message and leave. Other times, he would stay for hours and talk with her.

"What do you think about the 'Masses and the Ruling Power,' the editorial printed in the last issue of our newspaper?"

Mina thought the article was too harsh on Bazargan. It was too soon to criticize his government. He was different from the clergy.

"You are too optimistic! No, you should not trust the liberals. Neither Banisadr nor Bazargan. They will all serve the bourgeoisie's interests. Our collaboration with them is merely tactical," Mohsen said.

"But they are supported by the masses. We have to cooperate with them."

"Masses would support anyone Khomeini selects. You cannot trust any of them, neither the liberals nor the clergy."

"Radical Islam? What do you mean? You must have read Shariati's books!"

"Women's rights in Islam? Political freedom? These are all lip services. Shari'ati is another tie-wearing mullah! They don't believe in equality of men and women. Remember Khomeini's dispute with the Shah on the so-called White Revolution; he did not approve of granting women the right to vote and of the land reforms. Islam respects the ownership of land by feudalism and does not believe in the distribution of wealth. The religious far right could not even tolerate those mild bourgeois reforms."

Mina touched the wound on her forehead. Covered by a bandage, it was still painful.

"We only cooperated with them for a short time - while we all fought against the Shah and Imperialism - not anymore."

"The struggle is not over yet. The clergy have barely begun. Just wait and see what bloodshed they will start. They will first come after us, the Marxist organizations, and then go after other intellectuals."

"Don't think the Americans closed their eyes and failed to protect their puppet, the Shah, for no reason. The existence of a religious government in Iran will help the U.S. to defeat communists and leftists in the region. Americans first supported the Afghan's *mujahedin*, then Iran, and after that it could be Iraq, Syria, or Jordan."

"Dear comrade, don't be that optimistic. Just look at yourself in the mirror. They have already talking about stoning women! We have hard days in front of us."

"Armed struggle? No, that thesis is in question now. Our comrades started a just and fair armed struggle in *Siahkal* against Pahlavi regime. They did not have any other choice left, but look what happened to them."

"We should now start with the factories. The proletariat should first become aware of their rights."

Mohsen gave Mina missions to carry out, mostly trivial, rarely a significant one. Get the newsletters from Dr. Zahraee's office on Wednesdays. You are now in charge of distributing our newsletter in your workplace. Please collect contributions from your colleagues and give them to Mr. Mahmoodi. From now on, get

101

newspapers from Danesh bookstore. Enter from the back door and ask them for the books you ordered last week. Zary's organizing a strike at Cheat-e Ray textile factory. Take few days off from work. She needs your help.

"Next Thursday, after work, leave your car in front of the office and go home with a taxi. Leave the key on top of the left front tire." Her car was back in front of her house on Friday evening or early on Saturday morning, before she left for work.

Mina never figured out what Mohsen did for work. One day he would come to her house wearing a pair of clean, neat slacks and shirt, his beard shaved, and his hair neatly combed. Another day he would wear a suit, and yet another day, he would appear unshaven, with a dirty, muddy outfit, and soiled fingernails, as though he were an unskilled construction worker. Whatever he did, he knew how to keep Mina under his spell. She was growing fond of him.

• • •

Mina went to Dr. Zahraee's office every Wednesday evening. She met Mohsen there and collected pamphlets or newspapers to distribute in her office the next day, among the people who anxiously waited to get the news from Fadai Organization. By that time of night, the building was almost empty. Mohsen had the key; he usually came earlier and waited for her in the hall.

That night Mohsen was not in the hall. Had he been arrested? Mina panicked. The place could have been exposed. But nothing was out of place; everything looked the same. A big open space with modern furniture: a white leather sofa, two big black leather chairs, a white lacquered coffee table and two matching side tables.

The door to the doctor's office was slightly open. Mina, hesitantly, opened the door. Mohsen sat behind a big old desk, his head down, writing something. Mina had never been inside the room. It was dark and full of antiques. The room smelled strange.

Mohsen looked up, said hello, then got up and came to her. An unfamiliar smile covered his face. He held her hands in his big rough hands and kissed them. Mina was confused. He kissed her hands again. He pulled her closer and kissed her lips and neck, gently at first, then so passionately that his teeth pressed against her lips. Mina was still in shock. He inserted his hand into her bra touching her breast. Her bra's hook pushed to her skin and her lips burned.

Mohsen stopped abruptly, went back to the desk, and busied himself moving papers around. Mina escaped the room.

The next Wednesday Mina wondered if she should go to their appointment or not. What was the nature of their relationship now? Was he now her lover? Or he was her comrade? Her leader? A leader Mina obeyed just as she obeyed Parviz and Zary. Besides his friendly hug at their last meeting, Parviz had never tried to touch her body. She stayed home.

The week after, she was in Doctor Zahrai's office. She stopped at the door for a minute, closed her eyes and breathed in deep. She finally overcame her hesitation and went in.

Mohsen opened Mina's bra before touching her breasts. She did not pull back. He led her to the desk and kissed her again, even harder than before. While caressing her breast, he opened his fly. Mina stared in his eyes. A completely strange feeling washed over her, her heart pounding harder. Mohsen squeezed her tighter and kissed her neck and breasts. Her body was on fire. Mohsen turned her around on the desk, pushed her skirt up, and pulled her panties down. He laid on her back, rubbed his penis against her, casually at first. Mina could hear the sound of his breathing. Then he got agitated and frantic. His breathing got harder and harder. He mumbled some words in her ears. Mina felt the thrust of a warm, heavy fluid on the small of her back. He stayed atop of her for a moment, then withdrew himself and zipped up his fly. He fetched the Kleenex box from the side table and placed it next to Mina. Mina still lay on her stomach. Mohsen left the room without a word.

Mina's mind went entirely blank. She stayed motionless for a few minutes. Her back was wet. She drew a tissue from the box and cleaned herself, then pulled her panties up, covered herself with her skirt, and got off the table.

In the hall, Mohsen gave her a handful of pamphlets without looking in her eyes.

Before Mina left the office, Mohsen called out to her, "I am sorry. I didn't want... wasn't right... to do it..." He mumbled. Ashamed, Mina ran away. Why didn't she resist? Why had she let him go on? Should she be mad at him now? Should she hate *him* or herself? Was it a rape? No, he could not be a rapist. He was a leader;

thousands of people Mina valued respected him. She respected him. She was now part of his private life too, the private life of a Great Comrade.

The next few times that they were together, Mohsen still resisted penetrating her. Then Mina wanted him to. She did not care about her virginity anymore. Now she desired him too. She wanted to know how it felt to make love to someone. But even after that, sex felt the same. Nothing. Except shame and frustration. He penetrated her until he ejaculated, then left the Kleenex box next to her and left the room.

• • •

"Pregnant? Are you sure? Who said that?"

"The doctor, I am two months pregnant."

"Why didn't you say anything sooner? Two months? I don't think it is too late yet; you still can have an abortion. Go see the doctor again. Do it quickly."

Should she consult with Dr. Zahraee? Mina felt some chill. She hardly saw Dr. Zahraee or talked to her. Dr. Zahraee usually left office before it was dark. Mina and Mohsen met after dark. What should she tell her? Should she reveal her affair with Mohsen? What would Dr.Zahraee think of her if she did?

"Don't tell anyone about it," Mohsen started caressing her face and hair. "You should keep it a secret between us."

Mina could not stop her tears.

"Are you crying? Please don't act like a sentimental girl. You should abort the baby," Mohsen got serious. "You cannot afford it now. We have so many things to do. We have to concentrate on the Movement now. We have a real enemy against us." He wiped the tears from Mina's face. "Let's forget about it for now." He then kissed her lips.

After he had sex with her, Mohsen showed her a flyer. It was in black-and-white and hand-written. "Join us tomorrow morning at 9.00 am in front of the American Embassy on Takht-e-Jamshid, Persepolis, Avenue." One of the students, whom he knew from before revolution, had handed him the flyer on campus and had told him there might be a seizure of the Embassy. The group that had signed the flyer, The Muslim Students of the Imam Khomeini's Line, was unknown to Mohsen. Something seemed suspicious.

Before Mohsen opened the door to leave, he stopped, turned to Mina, began to say something but paused for a moment. He then went back to the desk and started playing with the papers. As he was about to leave, he finally asked, "how do you know I am the father of your child?" How did she know who the father of her child was? How did *she* know? Who else could be the father! Didn't he notice she was a virgin? Didn't he know he was the only man she had ever had sex with?

When Mina got home, Zary was waiting for her in front of her apartment. She too, had received the black and white flyer, and wanted to go to the embassy the next day. She stayed over, because Mina's home was close enough to the embassy to get there on time in the morning.

• • •

Nov. 4, 1979 / Aban 13, 1358

Mina and Zary hopped into a taxi and arrived to the American Embassy around 8:30. Takht-e-Jamshid Ave. seemed no different from any other day. People walked on the sidewalks, cars sped by and honked frequently. The shops and offices started to open. Mina glanced inside the open door of a bank. Two people lined up in front of a teller. A middle-aged woman stood talking to another teller. Everyone was running their daily errands.

Mina and Zary situated themselves in front of a newsstand not too far away from the embassy, and busied themselves by reading the headlines. When Mina leafed through the pages to read the rest of the news, the man at the counter looked at her in disappointment. "Miss, do you want to buy a Keyhan? It's just one toman."

One of the young men in front of the newsstand moved away while smiling bashfully at Mina. Mina, embarrassed, took one toman from her handbag and bought the newspaper.

From where they stood, Mina and Zary could see the concrete walls of the embassy and the tall pine trees peeking up above the them. The embassy's iron gate was locked with a heavy chain.

Shortly before 10.00 am, the student protestors arrived. Their angry outbursts could be heard minutes before they appeared.

Death to America
Death to Imperialism
Death to the Shah

Death to America and its chained dog
Death to America, Death to Carter

Then Mina saw them, the students. Some of the women in the group wore chadors, while the majority wore pants with long tunics and dark headscarves. The men, out-numbering the women, walked in the back rows. Most of them had beards and mustaches and wore military coats and armbands with the name of their group. Some also hung images of Ayatollah Khomeini on their torsos.

People stopped on both sides of the street to watch. No one chanted. Mina looked to see if Mohsen was there. He wasn't.

The Muslim students continued their walk toward the American embassy in a calm, orderly manner. They now had the full attention of the crowd. They stopped about a hundred meters before the gate. Mina saw one of the women take out a chain cutter from underneath her chador and give it to one of the two men who were guarding her. Another woman took out a long stick from underneath her chador and handed it to a man walking behind her. All three men rushed toward the embassy and started cutting the chains. Two more men reached the gate at the same time. They, too, carried wire cutters.

Zary and Mina walked closer. There was more than one chain locking the gate. When one group finished their work, they rushed to help the others until they had cut all the chains. Now the other members of the group joined them, pushing and pulling the gate, each time harder. It seemed the gate was locked from the inside.

Another group of young men, who stood behind,

hurried to the walls. They hooked their hands together, making rungs for other boys to climb. Two of then reached the top of the wall and jumped over into the embassy's garden. A few minutes later, the gate opened to the crowd.

The students chanted loudly: *Allahumaa Salli ala Mohammed wa aale Mohammed,* Allah's blessing be upon Mohammed and Mohammed's family.

People in the crowd repeated the chant: *Allahumaa Salli ala Mohammed wa aale Mohammed.*

The rest of the students streamed into the embassy, repeating their protest:

Death to America
Death to Imperialism
Death to the Shah
Death to America and its chained dog
Death to Carter

In a short while, Mina heard the sound of shooting from inside the embassy. The crowd moved back cautiously. Who was shooting? Was it protestors or the Americans? Zary walked toward the embassy, pulling Mina with her. When they arrived at the gate, Mina removed her hand from Zary's and stopped. Zary looked at Mina's serious expression with wonder, then turned away and left without saying goodbye. Mina stayed still and watched her go inside, shoulder to shoulder with other young men and women.

The street filled with people who had been standing on both sides of the street, and the traffic was in a total gridlock.

For quite some times, Mina anxiously waited to hear

news from inside the embassy. She finally walked away. A couple of streets away she flagged a taxi to go to work. It was the News time. The driver turned up the radio's volume:

"Today a group of young Islamic revolutionary students, who call themselves the Muslim Students of the Imam Khomeini Line, seized the American spy nest in Tehran to protest the ex-Shah's admittance to the United States, to stop the imperialist and Zionist conspiracies, and to make their voices heard by the people of the world."

That evening Radio Iran announced, Bazargan had resigned along with his cabinet, following the hostage taking.

The next week, Hossein called to say the Americans were talking about closing their borders to all Iranians.

What should she do now? Hossein always mentioned how easy it was to find a job in the United States. She could go to graduate school and keep the baby. Everybody would find out about her pregnancy, if a war started between the two countries and she could not make it to America soon.

Two weeks later Mina left Tehran in a hurry, without even going to Borazjan to say goodbye to her parents.

The trip to New York took her much longer than she expected.

• • •

Sept. 10, 2001 / 2:30 p.m.

"Ms. Shabani, would you like to have a

refreshment?" The flight attendant was back.

"Yes please. I'll have a piece of tiramisu if you still have one left, and a glass of pinot noir," said Mina.

"I'll have the same," ordered the passenger sitting next to her.

"It seems you, too, are fond of desserts," said Mina while eating her tiramisu.

"Yes, I am," said the man while glancing at her. "Oh, you have a piece of chocolate on your face!" He pulled himself close to Mina and wiped the chocolate off from the corner of her mouth with the tip of his finger. Mina watched him do it.

"May I invite you for dinner or a drink while you are in New York?" he asked her few minutes later.

Mina raised her eyes and looked at him with surprise, then held out her hand to him.

"My name is Mina: Mina Sha'abani."

"Oh...I am sorry. My name is John, John Myers. It's embarrassing, I asked you out, but I didn't even introduce myself!"

Mina's laughter had a playful, flirtatious tone.

"That's okay, Mr. Myers. Don't worry about it. Unfortunately, I am too busy tomorrow and I am not sure of my schedule for the rest of my stay," Mina said in a more serious tone.

"I understand, I understand. Please call me John," he said without any hard feelings.

"I travel to New York all the time," Mina said with a friendly smile. "If you give me your number, I will call you next time I am in town."

"That's great." John handed her one of his business cards.

Mina leaned her head on the chair and closed her eyes. She didn't want to have more distractions during the trip. She had the work meeting and Shirin to deal with.

She was hoping the meeting would be over before 6.00 pm, so she could go to the Top of the World at the top of the South Tower, her favorite place, to watch the sunset. It was a personal joy she tried not to deprive herself of. Every time she visited New York, if she didn't have to spend her free time on any of those bureaucratic, dull business dinners, which she often had to, she went to the Top of the World. She bought herself a glass of California Merlot and watched the beautiful narrow beams of sunlight going down in between Manhattan's skyscrapers.

Maybe this time she could convince Shirin to go to the Top of the World to watch the sunset with her.

Los Angeles - Birth

<u>Nov. 14, 1979</u>

"You gained so much weight!" said Hossein. He greeted Mina in LAX.

Mina bent forward slightly and crossed her arms in front of her stomach, "and you lost so much!" Mina said. "Mother wouldn't rest until she put ten kilos on your skinny body!"

"I miss her greasy food so much!" Hossein smiled and put Mina's luggage on his Yellow Cab. "We will be home in an hour; you can start fattening me then."

Except for the weight, Hossein had not changed much. He had the same wide, dark brown eyes and bushy eyebrows shadowing his eyes which looked softer now. He didn't look as much like Father as he did before.

A frail layer of fog made the city barely visible. Tall big buildings in different sizes and shapes appeared in front of their eyes, as Hossein changed one freeway to another. The buildings seemed mysterious and hard to approach.

"This is downtown, the heart of the city," explained Hossein. "Here is where the rich and poor come across."

Although extremely exhausted, Mina did not want to miss anything.

"That's Hotel Bonaventure," Hossein pointed to one of the more attractive structures. "I usually pick up my customers from there. It's the biggest and the most beautiful hotel on the west coast."

He even bragged about having a drink in the hotel's famous restaurant on the top floor. Hossein promised to take her there soon for dinner. A turning restaurant revealing the entire downtown landscape with its buildings and lights, must be interesting.

Hossein took Mina directly to his apartment, stayed only long enough to get the news about the family and went back to work. He had to work six days a week to survive. More than half of his income went to the cab owner.

Mina tried to take a nap, but after tossing and turning for more than an hour, she got out of the bed and started unpacking.

Although only a one bedroom apartment, the apartment had enough space to accommodate both of them. Could she also fit a small crib somewhere?

In the afternoon, a faded ray of sun came out from under the clouds, passed the big dirty window, and shone on the floor. Through the window, she could see a narrow backyard with a small pool in its center. No one was around the pool. She should wash the windows.

Mother wouldn't sleep in such a room until she cleaned everything and removed all the spots from the windows. But she was too tired to do any cleaning. Maybe the next day.

After an hour, the noise and the laughter of children brought her back to the window: three small kids with dark skin and dark hair, and a short, squat woman wearing shorts and pushing a small stroller yelling at the kids in an unfamiliar language. Before long, more children arrived. Along with the first set of children and their mothers, they filled the backyard with their noises and outcries. The building was even more crowded than the Iran Khanum's Hotel Sedaghat_e No on the Rahahan Square in Tehran.

• • •

How should she tell Hossein about her pregnancy? Can he understand? Will he get angry and start beating her? No, he wouldn't do that! He is much more open-minded now. He has a girlfriend. The girlfriend, a fake blond Salvadorian, was even talking about moving in with him.

Mina finally decided to talk to Hossein. She told him she had married one of her coworkers in Tehran.

"I didn't tell anyone in Borazjan," she said. "If I told Mother, she would've wanted me to go through all the rituals. You know how much I hate those traditions." She then added, "Mohsen will join me as soon as he can leave."

Mina's belly gradually grew so big that she could not cover it anymore. Hossein started to ask about Mohsen and his plans, but became suspicious when he heard conflicting stories. He then stopped asking and became reserved. He stayed at his girlfriend's apartment more often. He totally ignored the fact that Mina was pregnant.

Sometimes Mina went without any decent food at home for days. She needed to leave Hossein's home. She needed to work; her savings was not enough to support her. Hossein's girlfriend introduced her to a white American man.

"He found me a job when I first came here," she said.

What could she do? Engineering. Forget it. It is impossible for someone with no work permit, especially from Iran, to find an engineering job.

How about house cleaning? Babysitting? Could she wait tables? That was something she could do.

The man charged her two hundred dollars, and sent her for an interview to a medium size restaurant with big old synthetic leather furniture. The restaurant was part of a big chain, famous for having discounted prices for senior citizens. They had a sign for hiring a part time waitress on the window.

"Do you have any experience?" asked the manager. He had a heavy Indian accent.

"Yes, yes." The recruiter had advised Mina to say that. "I worked in a restaurant in Iran while I studied in college."

"In Iran? I didn't know girls waited in restaurants in Iran!"

Mina kept silent.

"Ok, it doesn't matter as long as you don't mention to the customers you are from Iran," said Mr. Kumar, the manager. "I pay you two dollars fifty cents an hour. Cash. You can make good tip from old folks if you serve them right."

Mina moved out of Hossein's apartment the next week.

Her new place was a tiny apartment, smaller than Iran Khanum's basement, not too far from the restaurant. Who cared? It was a safe place for her and the baby. She can work hard and take care of her child. Nobody could harm them anymore.

• • •

Mina rose from her right side, sat down on the bed for a moment, then laid back on her left side. When her belly was smaller, she put two pillows, one at each side, and slept on her stomach. Now she soon grew short of breathe and woke up. Her legs had swollen badly. The doctor advised her to walk every day. How could she walk after ten hours of work and serving more than fifty customers?

When Mother was pregnant, her abdomen never got as big as Mina's. Nane-ye Mohammad's was even smaller. They did not notice she was pregnant until a few months before she gave birth to her child. She worked until the last day of her pregnancy. Her last baby was born right after the spring-cleaning, two days before Nowruz. She did not come to work only on the first day after her delivery. The next day Nane-ye Mohammad was there at seven in the morning, working all day, nonstop. The little boy died in less than two months. She was probably happy after the death of her husband. No more suffering!

Mina got up from the bed and started pacing around the room. She still had a few more weeks. Working with those swollen legs was unbearable. The doctor insisted she should reduce her work hours. Sure, she would stay home a couple more hours, only if Mr. Kumar paid for the expenses of the childbirth, for the days she had to stay home after; and for the baby's formula and diapers. That asshole would probably even penalize her for those days!

The last doctor had advised her to bring her husband for the Lamaze class.

"My husband? Why?"

Because he could help her during her labor. They would teach him to help her with her breathing and when to push. Hah? What was he talking about? If Mother or Nane-ye Mohammad heard such a nonsense, they would pass out from laughter! Who had heard of a husband being present during childbirth? Mother said Father always left right after he brought the midwife home, and went to stay with his friends. He did not return until the late evening, or the next day, after the baby was cleaned and ready. Nane-ye Mohammad's husband did not even know when his wife was giving birth to one more mouth.

I am not married, she told the nurse. How about your boyfriend? The baby's father? No, I have not heard from him for a long time. A sister? A brother? No. I have no one.

She had not even heard from Hossein for a long time. She had called him and left messages a few times, but he had not returned her calls.

No news from Mohsen either. Mina could not even find Zary. Mahnaz didn't know where she was. Zary's phone rang and rang, and no one responded to the letters Mina sent her. Even if Mohsen wanted to contact Mina, he did not have her address. He had definitely tried to find her. How could he not?

• • •

She was still in bed when she first felt the pain. What a bad day! Wednesday was the senior discount day. The majority of her best customers came to the restaurant that day. Mina knew most of them by name and remembered their favorite foods. They usually requested to sit in her section, even those bastards Mr. and Mrs. Jones who constantly needed extra service and left little tip. Serving seniors also gave her a good opportunity to practice her English. They asked about everything. Where are you from? Afkanistan? Where is Afkanistan? Oh, yes. It is close to Eye-run. Close to Koomainie. Is this your first child? What does the baby's father do?

Baby's father...oh, yes, my baby's father... He is an engineer. He has a good job in Afghanistan. No, he not come here soon.

The pain started from deep under her stomach, a sharp, quick pain; first in one-hour intervals, then half an hour, and then shorter. The sting of pain got sharper and stronger on the bus on her way to work. She couldn't sit still; she got out of the bus two stops, before her usual stop.

Two of her favorite customers had just arrived when

the pain began to come every fifteen minutes. Mr. Adams was a funny, jolly grayed-hair gentleman. He always brought a smile to Mina's face. His wife, Mrs. Adams, was also a kind-natured woman who laughed hard at all of Mr. Adams's jokes and remarks. They always left her a generous tip.

Mina took a carafe of coffee to their table before they asked for it. "Good morning!"

"Good morning Sunshine. How is it going?"

"Very vell tankiyou, just this baby kicking harder."

"He must be tired of that dark, confined place."

They always referred to the baby as 'he'. They probably thought, being from the Middle East, Mina would prefer to have a boy.

"Oh, yes, especially in a beautiful day like this. I am sure she wants to meet two beautiful person like you. What can I get you?"

She was taking their order when her water broke. "Aakh…" She placed the coffee pot on the table.

Mr. and Mrs. Adams looked at her with concern. Mr. Adams helped her to sit. "Do you want us to take you to the hospital?" asked Mrs. Adams.

Mina shook her head vaguely.

"Do you want us to inform anybody?" asked Mr. Adams, now sitting next to her. "Your brother? Your sister? How about any friend?"

"Oh no, no need for that, they are all busy, no, it is ok." Tears came to her eyes.

Pain spread all over her body. Her underwear and skirt were entirely wet.

"Please take me to UCLA Harbor hospital. It is not far. They have my records."

The backseat, where Mrs. Adams led Mina to lay down, got spotted with her water. Their car was as clean as they both were. Mina should do something for them, she now owed them. The next time they come to the restaurant, she would serve them with their favorite dessert. They ordered Ice cream Sundays only on special occasions. She will not put it on the bill. Fuck Mr. Kumar.

Mrs. Adams sat next to Mina at the hospital, and held her hand while wiping her tears with a napkin. She was parting from the waist; someone pulled her legs while another one pulled her arms. Maybe the stupid baby did not know how to exit her body? Oh...no, NO. Please let me alone. Let me go home. I will come back tomorrow. I promise. NO, I can't bear it anymore; I can't do it today. Please, please let me go. Let me alone. No, no, no...

A moment of quietness. What a relief! Her body went numb. No more pain.

"It's a girl! Congratulations. A beautiful baby girl!"

A girl? A beautiful girl? Why is she not crying? The pain came back to her heart. Is she ok? I want to know. Please let me know! Please somebody tell me. Is she OK? Are her legs healthy? Her arms? Her eyes? Will she be able to walk some day? The image of Zahra dragging her legs marched in front of Mina's eyes.

• • •

Hello Mr. Jones, how are you today? Oh. Yes, I am fine. Yes, I am smiling again. Would you like more coffee? More? Sure! More? More? ...Yes Mrs. Jones, I know, I know, Mr. Jones like his coffee warm. Tankiyou, baby is fine. Tankiyou for asking. It is kind of you. Oh, yes, yes she is growing; she is saying some words now. No, no I don't have a good picture of her with me. Sure, sure, I will bring it next time. Yes, yes Mrs. Peterson, I know you like your butter on the side. Sorry, I will change your toast again. Ok, I will make it darker too. Of course, don't worry. I am here to serve you. I do anything to get a tip from you. Your tip... Tankiyou Mr. Matteyous. Tanks! Yes Mrs. Matteyous, I know. Mr. Matteyous is very generous. Yes, his one dollar will do a lot for me! Yes, a lot. It will help me to survive. Help me not to die. Not to die from hunger. It is enough to buy an old loaf of bread from the bakery outlet for my breakfast, or spend it for my baby's diaper... Yes Mr. Kumar! I am coming. Just a minute Mr. Kumar, I am on my way to table 5. Yes, Mr. Kumar, fuck you Mr. Kumar. Fuck you. Fuck you... fuck all of you. Fuck you, Mr. Jones, go fuck yourself and that chatty wife of yours. Fuck the baby, fuck the pictures... You want more coffee for Mr. Jones? Ok Mrs. Jones, here is the warm coffee. Here is a full carafe of coffee... you can have it all...

She emptied the entire pot in Mr. Jones's cup.

• • •

Why does this child smile so much? She smiles even when she has a high fever. She smiles if you only glanced at her.

Oh no, not now. I am not in the mood to play with you. I don't want to see those dimples of yours. They resemble Mohsen's. Where the hell is he now? Why is he not finding us? She had told him that she was pregnant. Didn't she? Yes she did. But he denied it was his child. *How does she know who the father of the child is?* Didn't he really believe her? Or was it just his way of not accepting any responsibility? If he sees Shirin, he definitely would believe her; the same eyes, the same dimples, the same dark hair.

• • •

Her legs were so tired she could hardly move, and yet she had to cook Shirin's supper and prepare her lunch for the next day; it was too expensive to buy baby food. Mina didn't have to cook for herself. The one free meal she ate at the restaurant was enough. She usually ate her lunch later in the day so she wouldn't get hungry at night. It was healthier anyway. It was even better for keeping her in shape! She had lost twenty pounds since the baby was born. She had not gained even half of that during her pregnancy. She was pale and frail. Are you sick? No, I am not. Vitamin deficiency? Maybe. Calcium deficiency? That too, but these were not what kept her awake at night. She needed money. She couldn't afford to spend money on such trivial matters. She needed the money for rent, for gas and electricity, for baby's formula and diapers, and most of all, for the babysitter. This month she should save even more. It had been more than two months since she had called Mother. Mother must be very worried now. Each telephone call to Borazjan cost her at least ten dollars. Ten dollars was just enough to cover the call if she could hang up before finding out how Mother's knee pain was, or how much

Father's blood pressure had gone up, or if Nane-ye Mohammad was still alive, or if Mahnaz visited them enough.

Hello Mother. How are you? ...I am fine, too...I am great... everything's ok.

Oh yes, I have enough money to live on for a while. You shouldn't be worried about me...

Hossein... oh yes, he is ok. I just talked to him yesterday. Yes, Mother. I have finished my master's degree. No, I am not in the mood to work on my doctorate degree, I know I told you last time that I would do that, but this degree is enough for now.

She had to hang up before Mother asked more, and she had to lie more. "I love you maman, I have to go. I am late for work... I can't talk to baba now I have to go... I will call you... I promise... kiss him for me too."

Here it went ten dollars! Here it went four hours of work! The four hours she could sleep and rest instead.

• • •

It was almost dark when Mina got home. Three young men stood in front of the building. They stopped talking and stared at her as she appeared, their eyes full of disgust and hatred. Mina had seen them before. They all lived on the floor above her. They muttered some words as she passed them. *Shit Iranian.* She rushed to her door. A week earlier one of them had shut the gate in front of her so hard, that it nearly hit her in the face.

• • •

"What do you mean by you cannot come to work today? This is the third time in the past two weeks. I won't put up with it anymore," Mr. Kumar yelled.

"Shirin is sick," Mina mumbled.

"She is sick again? Find someone to take care of her."

"I have to take her to a doctor. Please find someone else for today."

"No, I can't find anyone to cover for you today," Mr. Kumar got aggravated. "I should have fired you the last time you called." He paused for a second: "I will fire you if it happens again."

"She had fever all last night," Mina begged desperately. "I cannot leave her with the babysitter today."

"...It is not my fault that she had a fever all night! I need you today. I don't have anyone to cover for you again!"

Mina heard the sound of the receiver slamming down. She was not worried about losing her job. Where could Mr. Kumar find a waitress as cheap and as hard working as she was? A server who was willing to work any shift he gave her.

She must take Shirin to a doctor. She had a fever for the past forty-eight hours. The free clinic was not far, but it would take her at least two hours to get there by bus - three lines, each twenty five minutes, half an hour in the bus stop waiting for the next bus to arrive, and then a couple more hours waiting in the clinic.

As she opened the door, something kept the door from opening entirely. She peeked outside. A thin, narrow rope stopped the door. The ends of the rope were nailed to the wall on each sides. A piece of paper with a note in red magic marker faced her: "Iranians are all pigs."

The rope tore apart as Mina pushed the door open. She poked her head out and carefully inspected the hallway. Her eyes went to the dark, narrow staircase going up in front of her. It must be those three boys living on the top floor. Frightened, she shut the door and locked the bolt.

Mina gave up the idea of taking Shirin to the doctor. What if they were waiting for them downstairs? She could not deal with them or anyone anymore. She had had enough. She would just stay home and take care of her baby. She *must* stay home. She must quit her job too. She would not leave Shirin with the babysitter anymore. How did she know the babysitter wouldn't starve Shirin to death? Wasn't she very hungry last week when Mina picked her up? She might even lock Shirin up and let her cry all day. She remembered how one time Shirin's eyes were red and swollen when she brought her back home.

• • •

Sunday, Sept. 3rd, 1983

My dearest Mahnaz, Salaam;

I have missed you and everybody else so much. It is more than three years since I have seen your kind eyes. I never imagined that remembering your lively eyes would be my only hope and happiness in life. You don't know how much I have missed you. I've missed everybody, especially Mother. How is she doing? I know I have not called her in the past couple of months. I have been thinking of you and her, every day and wished I could call.

I lied to Mother about seeing Hossein. I am not a good liar, he doubted the story I had made up about Shirin's father. He doesn't talk to me anymore. I am so thankful that you did not show much curiosity about Shirin. I will tell you all about it, when I come back. You are the only one I can trust with my secrets. Now, just think about me having a daughter, who is your niece, is as sweet as her name, and whose eyes are as beautiful as yours.

Please don't tell Mother and Father about Shirin. I am sure they would ask me hundred questions. I don't want to give them more lies. I am sure if they guess the truth, they will disown me. I can't bear something like that now. I can't bear Mother's heartbreak and Father's anger toward her.

The situation is not good here. I have never spoken of it over the phone. American people blame us for the hostage taking in Iran. I am sure my upper floor neighbors think Shirin and I personally arrested several of the embassy employees, tied them up with ropes, and took them to an Islamic guard station! Seriously, most Iranians here are worried about the Americans' revenge. Some people swore to God they saw a banner in a chain Pizza shop that said, "Have an Iranian for Thanksgiving." It means BBQ an Iranian instead of a turkey and eat it on Thanksgiving day, or something like this. I am not sure if it is true or just a made-up story. There is also a rumor about Reagan signing a law to allow the imprisonment of Iranians in concentration camps and the confiscation of their belongings. They did the same thing to the Japanese during WWII.

I don't even dare to take Shirin to the babysitter anymore. She is a Japanese-American woman who lives in my building. I made a mistake and told her we are Iranian and she told the other neighbors. My boss at the restaurant asked me to tell customers I am an Afghan. People here don't know us or Iran well. You can't imagine how many times people asked me about camel riding! Or if I had ever worn jeans before coming here, or whether I could go to college there. Questions like these. I am tired of it all. I am sure if I die one day, my boss Mr. Kumar would be the only one who would miss me! I want to come back home. I miss my workplace, my friends, my books, you, Mother and Father. I even miss Borazjan and its dirt roads and narrow alleys. Sometimes I wonder if I could one day feel those awful sandy winds and humid weather on my skin again! You knew how much I hated them when I lived there. I even miss Nane-ye Mohammad and her children, Mohammad and Zahra. Is she still alive? Who is taking care of Zahra?

What do you think about my coming back to Iran with Shirin? Sometimes I dream that Mother and Father have moved to Tehran, and Mother is taking care of Shirin. I know it is too much to ask. Maybe I can find a trustworthy nanny to take care of her while I am at work. I would love to hear you reciting your beautiful poems to me. We could go to poetry readings, cinemas, and cafeterias, drink coffee, and have hot intellectual discussions.

Do you think I can get my old job back? I have not resigned from my job; I just got a two-year vacation without pay. Technically, I am still their employee. Please write me as soon as possible, and let me know what you think about the idea of my coming back. I have to get an Iranian birth certificate for Shirin and add her to my passport. I don't know what to do if they ask me for her father's documents. Shirin's American birth certificate just shows me as her mother. Here they don't bother if she has no official father. You don't need to worry about this stuff; I will find a way to take care of it. You just tell me to come, and I will fly to you.

How are you doing with your poetry book? Have you found a publisher yet?

With much love.
Your lonely sister, Mina

• • •

She should contact Mohsen. If only she could send him a picture of Shirin he would be convinced Shirin is his daughter. Nobody could deny the resemblance. He would not abandon his child.

When she first came to the US, Mina got to know some members of the Student Supporters of the Democratic Movement in Iran. They must be in touch with the activists in Iran. Maybe they could help her find either Zary or Mohsen.

The Student Supporters Group had rented a room from the supporters of the Nicaraguan Socialist Revolutionaries, the Sandinistas. They had the room two evenings a week in downtown LA, to hold their cultural gatherings and study groups. Mina had gone there when her belly was not that big, when she still had a small amount of time to spend on the things she liked to do. Mina still had a phone number for Parvaneh, one of the students.

No, she did not know anyone by those names. However, a comrade was coming from Europe for a lecture. She had fled Iran less than a year ago; she might know Mohsen or Zary.

Mina went to her lecture in downtown. A young man, along with a young woman, searched her handbag and Shirin's diaper bag. The narrow tables in the hallway were covered with pamphlets and underground newsletters coming from Iran.

The Islamic regime had detained quite a number of revolutionaries, particularly the leftists. Many had to flee the country. The prisons were full of high school and college students, who were arrested for distributing pamphlets, selling newsletters, or just supporting a political organization. The most terrifying news was about the mass executions of the political prisoners by Islamic regime in less than six months.

Mina found a vacant chair in the back row and sat. The room was quite packed. There were many pictures of Nicaraguan revolutionaries hanging from the walls along with some posters of the martyrs of Iranian political groups. In front of Mina, a big banner inscribed with red ink read:

What has happened to my country
That the prisons are filled with tulips and dew
And the survivors of the martyrs,
Like scattered masses of clouds, weep in the

wake of scorched tulips?

Under the banner was a picture of the poet Saeed Soltanpour. Mina remembered his black bushy mustache from his poetry reading in the Goethe Institute in Tehran. She did not know the people in the other pictures.

Shirin couldn't sit still. She ran between the rows of chairs and played with the audience. She went to anyone smiling to her.

"*Salam*. My mommy is here."

"I am three."

"My name is Shirin."

"Me? No I am not sweet, my name is Sweet."

"Mommy, Mommy, that lady asked me who my daddy is."

She made everybody smile. Mina had to get up many times to go through the rows and fetch her.

Someone was reading an article about ways to make connections with the proletariat in Iran. Shirin ran toward her. Before Mina could get her, Shirin smashed into one of the tripods holding pictures, in front of the stage. The picture fell down. Mina got a chance to look at the picture before she put it back. Mohsen! The same large boned face and the receding hairline, and that serious, dominant look in his eyes. How similar his chin and dimple were to Shirin's! Above the picture were the words: The great comrade, martyr Ali Mohammad Asgharzadeh (Comrade Mohsen).

Mina grabbed Shirin and they went back to their seats.

Soon everybody rose and applauded for the distinguished speaker entering the room.

Long live Fadaees
Long live revolutionaries
Long live Fadaees
Long live...

Shirin looked at the crowd in surprise and started clapping and repeating some of the slogans. The crowd finally stopped chanting and sat down. Shirin continued clapping and repeating words. Mina hugged her harder while wiping the tears off her own face.

The speaker, a tall woman with big bones, covered her head and part of her face with a Palestinian checkered shawl. She wore a pair of jeans and a green military jacket. The person seating at Mina's right whispered, "her husband was one of the highest-ranked members of the organization."

"They both were in prison in the Shah's regime," said the woman sitting at Mina's left. "Her husband was killed in a street fight with *Passdaran*."

"No, the Passdaran captured him in the fight. He killed himself by swallowing a cyanide pill he had hidden under his tongue, on the way to prison."

Mina felt empathy for the speaker. She might have a child like Shirin, a child who had never seen her father. Mina wanted to put her head on the woman's shoulder and weep with her.

When everybody fell silent, the woman started talking, her strong loud voice harmonized with her appearance. She talked about the similarities between the two regimes, the Shah's and Khomeini's, and the mistreatment of political prisoners in Iran. The crowd got up again, their fists above their head, and chanted:

Long live political prisoners
Salute to political prisoners
Political prisoner, you are our hero

When her speech ended, she walked along the pictures. Every time she mentioned a picture and the name, the crowd rose and chant, "Salute martyr..."

When she got to Saeed Soltanpour, the crowd's excitement peaked. He was arrested on his wedding night, taken to the prison and was executed shortly after.

After she was done introducing the other photographs, she pointed to Mohsen. She stared at him briefly: "The great comrade Mohsen." Her voice was trembling. Before the crowd started to shout his name, she sadly said, "my martyred husband." The crowd, full of emotion, gave her a long standing-ovation.

Salute to the great comrade Mohsen
Salute to our hero, comrade Mohsen
Salute to the martyrs

Shirin cheerfully mocked the crowd: "Saloo comrade Mosen."

"Grea..."

Mina's Revolution

Los Angeles - Shirin

<u>Dec. 1983</u>

Two hours past noon, and Mina was still in bed. She peeped through the opening between the bedroom and the rest of the apartment. The room was half-dark. Good. She could not see those ugly, aggressive orange spots covering the brown carpet. How many times had she tried to get rid of them? She had used different cleaners. No success. They grew bigger into a deeper orange. She had even dyed couple of spots. It made them disgusting.

Her eyes wandered around. An old sofa; her first purchase from visiting a garage sale. A small black and white 13-inch television sitting on a wooden side table covered with an Isfahan's *ghalamkar* tablecloth; her biggest gain in a flea market. Posters of Iranian sites of historical or geographical importance hanging on the walls next to the door; Persepolis; *Si o Se Pol*; the Damavand peak north of Tehran. Wasn't she proud of her heritage and the beauty of her country? The wall next to the kitchen was full of other kinds of posters, comrade Jazani in a suit and tie; comrade Ahmadizadeh with his beret; and a poem from Marzie Oskoee about being a proud revolutionary woman. A small shelf full of books she had brought from Iran separated the kitchen from the room. Can any of those help her?

She turned to her right and faced a half broken dresser next to the bed, Mahnaz's letter still sitting there since the previous day. The top and bottom of the letter were inscribed with Sa'di's poems. How much she missed Mahnaz! How fun were those summer days when they played together in that small room at the corner of the backyard regardless of Mother's shouts, regardless of the heat and the humidity. They could dress Shirin together and put their breasts in her mouth the same way they did with their dolls in that room. In their imaginary acts, their kids played together while Mina and Mahnaz cooked delicious food in their imaginary kitchens with imaginary ingredients. "Taste this," they'd say, smiling.

Tears dropped from the corner of her eyes before she burst out weeping for a long time.

As her weeping turned into a quiet sobbing, she looked around the room again. Rage filled her immediately. She rose from the bed, wiped the tears from her face, went to the posters, and tore them forcefully from the wall.

• • •

خبرت خرابتر کرد جراحت جدایی
چو خیال آب روشن که به تشنگان نمایی

My dearest sister, my Mina, Salam;
It is so hard to describe how happy I was to receive your letter, and how worried I got when I read it. This is the first time you are opening up about your difficulties.

What made you wait so long to write me about your pains, your troubles, and at the same time about the sweetness of your Shirin? Didn't you love me enough, or didn't you trust me enough to share your secrets? Who is the father of my dearest niece? Is he Iranian or American?

Two months ago, when you first told me about Shirin on the phone, I thought you were teasing me, or I heard it wrong. You spoke vaguely and hung up quickly.

Since I got your letter I have wrote some poems for you two, specifically for Shirin; for a girl whose aunt has never seen her but whose face is always in her mind. A little Mina who speaks English! Does she know Farsi too? I already miss you both.

I have not told Mother about your secret. Doesn't she have enough troubles and pains of her own? Let her be happy that she has a daughter who is working on her PhD and a son who had completed his education and has a successful Transportation Agency in America.

Please forget about coming back home in this situation.

گر غصه روزگار گویم	بس قصه بی شمار گویم
یک عمر هزارسال باید	تا من یکی از هزار گویم

Since you left, the situation has changed a lot. Even we, who are going through these changes day by day, cannot digest them; I don't know how *you* would be able to do it. Just imagine that it is forty degrees of centigrade, and you are wearing a black scarf and a long, dark coat, and waiting under a burning sun for a taxi that might not even pick you up because of your hair showing. Believe me, under those scarves and coats, it is much hotter and more humid than in Borazjan and under its burning sandstorms.

Hijab and Islamic dress code are strictly enforced. All female employees are required to wear *maghnea,* to make sure their hair is all covered. Guards stand at the entrance of offices to check women's nails and makeup. The taxis and restaurants hesitate to let in women who have "unsatisfactory hijab," meaning they have only covered their heads with scarves instead of *maghnea* and worn pants and long loose tonics without chador. Poetry readings, poetry nights and poetry clubs have disappeared. You can't believe such misery. I have hidden the drafts of my poems in a storage, never mind thinking of publishing them!

Don't be optimistic about retaining your old job. The new managing board of the company has fired you and most of your old colleagues. Don't even think about finding a new job. I am sure they have lots of information about you and your past political involvements. I did not want to give you the news; I am just telling you this now to make sure you do not come back. More than half of the Engineering department of your company and the other people you know have been imprisoned, including Dr. Zahraee. Mr. Mahmoodi got

executed three weeks ago, so was your friend Ezat
Tabaian, and several others. I am sorry to give you this
horrible news in this way. Over here we are getting used
to this kind of news. Most of the other activists who have
not been jailed yet are either hiding or have fled the
country.

Evin and Ghezel Hesar prisons are full again, most
of the prisoners are young students. Many of those who
helped us free the Shah's political prisoners, were locked
up in the same prisons; some of them might have been
executed already. We heard all kinds of things through
rumors.

This damn bloody war has stopped everybody's life. No
one can say anything; any complaint means you are a
traitor or a supporter of America. Many of the Toodeh
party's members have joined the Islamic army and gone
to fight against Iraq. They call it a war against
Imperialism, a war against Saddam, the puppet of
America. They believe they are supporting the deprived
masses!

You mentioned Nane-ye Mohammad, poor woman, she
still constantly scratches her body. I think every time she
does that, she loses pieces of her being. A few months
ago when Mother was sick and I went to Borazjan I saw
Mohammad. Please don't be worried about Mother, she
is fine now. I saw Mohammad standing at a corner of
Prison Square. He had on an army overcoat and army
boots; his nonmilitant shirt was loose over his pants, his
beard long and bushy. That is the attire of the Hezbollah
these days. He is a part of the neighborhood Islamic
committee. Mother had asked me not to appear in front
of him, because he might make trouble for us or even try

to frame us. I also saw your old friend, Maryam Aliabadi. I could not believe it was her; she looked so old you can't recognize her. Her hair mostly grey; her teeth decayed, or missing. Mother and I went to see her. Maryam's parents passed away last year. She and her husband are back in the same old house in our neighborhood. Do you remember that house? Just on the corner of the alley. The first day I got to Borazjan I saw two *hedjlehs*, for honoring her two martyred sons, in front of her home. Their corpses were brought back from the war zone to town the week before. She is not even thirty-five yet but has two martyred sons. Or, to be precise, she *does not have* two martyred sons! Poor baby, she cried and wept, and scratched her face so much that her voice and face were unrecognizable. You can't believe she is the same girl who was the clown of the class and could not stop mocking people or making them laugh.

No, my dear, please don't come back. Tolerate your situation in whatever way you can and be grateful that you are not here. Coming back is not going to solve your problems.

If Mother knew about Shirin, she would die from sorrow and shame. I don't want to think about what Father would do. Don't lose your hope in Hossein. Try to contact him again. You are expecting too much from him. Just remember he is a man who grew up in a culture where if a girl is not virgin they could behead her to preserve their honor! Do you recall when we were kids Father used to take us to the village of Deh Namaky? Do you remember how much fun we had? You, Hossein and I? We played all day with the village kids. Poor kids, they thought we were big shots, coming from Borazjan!

Recently a woman was stoned to death there. They said she had cheated on her husband. The official mullah of the village was the one to throw the first stone. Everybody in Borazjan talked about her. Father disagreed with stoning, but he didn't have any problem with hanging her! Our father who never believed in religion or its rules.

Have no doubts because of trouble
nor be thou discomfited;
For the water of life's fountain
 springeth from a gloomy bed;

Because of years of living in Tehran and then in America, you might have forgotten all of these. I hope Hossein has changed too. I am sure he has, but probably not as much as he should. You should be kinder to him. I know it is hard, but try to understand him. It is not his fault. It is all about this damn religious culture of ours; even if you are an intellectual, the honor of your sister and mother still is your honor and your value. I am sorry if I am lecturing you.

Does Hossein have a transportation firm as he told Mother? He wrote to Mother that he is doing very well and offered to send money to help them. Fortunately, Father has his pension and they have a paid off house in Borazjan. In Tehran, the cost of living and the rent have gone through the roof.

Please write me more. Send me a picture of your little sweetie. I can't wait to see her. I will send you all the poems I have written about you two whenever it becomes a full notebook.

The night is long and the hope to see the morning keeps me vigilant.
May it be that the breeze of the morning brings me your scent.
I wonder why the love`s roots doesn't bear fruit.
Though with a rain of enthusiasm I shower it.

Your faithful sister,
Mahnaz

• • •

Mina looked at the clock on top of the television. 2:30 am. Mahnaz's letter was in her hand, Shirin on her lap. She dropped the letter to the side of the bed, nestled Shirin on some pillows, and went to the bookshelf. She picked The Mother by Pearl Buck, which she had bought right before she left Tehran to read on the plane. She browsed through it, then closed her eyes and breathed deeply. She opened her eyes, looked at the book again, then threw it aside angrily. The book hit the door and fell on the floor next to the torn up posters, its pages open. Shirin opened her eyes, looked vacantly at Mina and went back to sleep.

Mina got up, went to the bathroom quietly and scrutinized herself in the mirror. Her face was pale with black spots all over it, a souvenir of her pregnancy. The mark of the old wound above her right eyebrow looked darker. She touched it; it felt swollen now. Her disheveled hair fell on her shoulders, her breasts were loose, her belly big. How old had she become! She could compete with Maryam - just like the old days when they competed to be first in their class, or to get Miss Ahmadi's attention. Now they could rival over who has become Miss Miserable.

She returned to the room. The dim light coming through the dusty window and its ragged covering made the room look more disgraceful. She opened the window and glanced outside. The house on the other side of the street and the sycamore trees in front of it were decorated with small colorful light bulbs blinking at short intervals.

Mina could see a white inscription over the black asphalt under the street light. She squinted, and read it suspiciously:

Go home you filthy Iranian

She closed the window quickly and turned away. Her eyes fixed on the stove in the corner of the room. It wouldn't take more than a few minutes. She should just open the gas valve and put her head inside the oven. Fast and painless, she had seen it in a movie. The woman in the movie, in a moment of despair, turned the gas valve on, opened the oven door, and poked her head into it. In a few minutes, her lifeless body lay next to the stove, calm and peaceful. Later, when the woman's daughters came back from school, they found her dead.

Mina returned to the bed. Shirin slept serenely, her breathing steady. Now that she wasn't smiling, her face resembled Mahnaz more than Mohsen. The same round face and long eyelashes. No, Shirin should not find her in that situation. At the end of the movie the woman's

143

daughter, by then a young lady, tried to kill herself the way her mother did.

Would they send Shirin to Iran? Or to an orphanage? A little Iranian orphan girl; a good target for revenge.

Pig. Pig. Little pig! Pig. Pig. Little pig!

Would they send her to a detention camp along with the rest of the Iranians?

Go home you filthy Iranian, go home, go home...

Go home?! Where is Shirin's home? If this is not *her* home, where else could be her home? Shirin doesn't have *a home*. She was born secretly; she had no father, no homeland, nobody. How about Mina? Wasn't Mina born lawfully? Yes, she was lawful indeed. She was a legal, a legitimate child according to all national, international, and religious laws accepted by all countries. Why didn't *she* have a county? Why couldn't *she* find a homeland? Wasn't she willing to work to death? She didn't expect much: only a comfortable home for her and her daughter, and enough food for their souls and bodies, a few free hours a day to read books, go to the movies and spend time with her loved ones. Was this too much? If she had made a mistake... wait a minute, *she* had made a mistake? What mistake? Being in love? Being passive? Being bashful? Mina had not even enjoyed the love making! Why should Shirin have to pay for it? Oh no, Mina was not going to leave her alone, oh no, not in that way. If Mina died, Shirin would remain alone in the apartment for days, and then she would die from hunger and horror. Police would discover them both. Maybe the Japanese lady in the lower level would inform the police. "There is an ugly smell coming from those Eye-ranian's apartment." She would certainly think Mina and Shirin were in the process of making a chemical bomb to blow up the entire neighborhood! Or maybe when the boys on the top level came to write another nasty slogan on her door, they would discover the smell of their decaying bodies. Then they could brag to other boys that they had killed them themselves. They might even get a trophy and become the heroes of the neighborhood for getting rid of those filthy dangerous terrorists. The police would inform the Iranian Consulate after they found her passport in the drawer. What would Mother say and feel? And the rest of the family? It would certainly be broadcast in the news. The newspapers would publish pictures of Mina and Shirin wearing these ragged clothes and living in this wretched apartment. People would talk about her: the breakdown of a girl who wanted to discover the world! Mother would regret letting her go to Tehran. Father would blame Mother for it. I *told you! Didn't I tell you Tehran is not a suitable place for a girl*? Yes, he had said a girl would be fooled and would create scandals and disgrace the family. Mother would regret not insisting on Mina getting married to Morteza or Bahram. Morteza would be happy; the uncles' wives would be happy too. They all had told Mother. A girl who goes to a big city alone would become bad and her destiny would be committing suicide in a dirty poor neighborhood of Los Angles, with a bastard child.

What had happened to her dreams of America? She had not achieved even one of her dreams. Not even the most insignificant and the pettiest one. She had not even had a day to enjoy her daughter, or to see her happy. Didn't Shirin deserve to have at least one happy day in her life?

• • •

Three hundred fifty-six dollars. She counted the money one more time; her tips, the money she had saved for rent and utilities. Usually she made more. But after the coffee incident, after she poured the entire coffee carafe on Mr. Jones's mug, many customers, the early-bird-discount-for-senior-citizens customers, preferred not to sit in her serving area, or if they did, they would leave her a small tip. Mr. Kumar had served Mr. and Mrs. Jones free lunches for the entire week, and had deducted the cost from Mina's wages.

Mina grabbed her savings booklet from under the mattress and put it in her purse with the cash. She went to the closet, a thrift store's treasure. The two pairs of shoes were real steals. Both flat heels and a size too large for comfort. She still had some of the outfits she brought from Iran: a pair of jeans, two loose blouses she used to wear to the demonstrations, a simple skirt and two shirts, one white, the other one blue, and some fancier clothing from the first years she started to work in Tehran, all too small for her now.

Shirin's wardrobe was as bad; she did not have any decent clothes either. Mina had never even bought her a nice toy or taken her to an amusement park where most kids went. They had eaten at McDonald's and Burger King only three times, despite the fact that Shirin repeatedly begged Mina to take her there.

Mina had always looked down on Mother; a woman who spent all her time just making a home and mothering. Now she wished she could do the same for Shirin.

It was 6.00 am. She had not slept most of the night, but she didn't feel sleepy. Surprisingly she even felt relaxed. No sign of anxiety. What a good feeling! She didn't have to wake Shirin up in the early morning, dress her and take her to the babysitter. She did not have to put up with Mr. Kumar's stupid face and stupid accent all day. She went back to bed.

• • •

"Mom I am thirsty; wake up; I am thirsty."

Mina opened her eyes; Shirin stood next to the bed touching her arm. Mina looked at the clock. Twenty past nine. No! She rushed out of the bed. Wait a minute! I *do not have* to go to work today! She could spend all her day with Shirin. Something she had never done.

Her happy thought flickered for a moment. Would she be able to make her plan work? Why not? She had to stop thinking and start acting on it.

Mina held Shirin tight in her arms, gave her a glass of water and then they went back to bed. She was content. It was a long time since she felt that way. Shirin looked very happy too. Mina played with her hair, her nose, tickled her belly and kissed her face all over. They played together in bed for the first time ever.

"Okay baby, it's another day. Let's take a shower first; we need a real nice shower this morning."

After a lengthy shower, she went through her

wardrobe again. She picked a couple of pieces and went back to the bathroom and tried them on one by one. She finally picked a white blouse and a black skirt; a more proper outfit than the others.

It wasn't ten thirty yet when they left home. Shirin was hungry. There was a McDonald's next to the bank. She passed it every day. They went in. She ordered an egg and sausage sandwich with hash browns for Shirin and a coffee for herself. Shirin could not sit still in one place. Every so often, she would get up from her chair and go to the other tables. This was the second time Mina noticed how easy and friendly she was with strangers. She smiled and said hello to every homeless and jobless person in the restaurant.

They got to the bank at eleven thirty. Now that she was not in a rush, unlike the other times, there was no line in front of the teller.

"Good morning!" Even the teller was friendly. She was not the same sullen, moody teller she usually got.

Mina handed her the saving booklet, "Good morning. I would like to get all my money."

"All five hundred dollars?" the teller looked at the booklet. "You have to leave some money there to keep the account open."

"That is ok, you can close the account. I don't need it anymore."

On her way out she shredded the booklet and tossed it in the garbage can. A few steps further, she entered a public phone booth and dialed the operator, "Operator, please connect me to the Hotel Bonaventure..." and deposited the thirty five cents that operator had asked for.

"Hotel Bonaventure? Yes, yes, I want a room for tonight, a room on your top floor."

"How much!? No, thanks, that is too expensive. Do you have anything cheaper?"

"Tenth floor is not too bad. How much with the tax and everything?"

"That is ok."

"No, I pay cash."

"Ok, I will be there before six. Thank you."

• • •

Mina glanced down the window. The people and cars looked smaller. The left side building was under the window and the right side one at least ten stories above it.

Shirin sat on the floor playing with the teddy bear Mina had bought her earlier. In the pink lacy dress and colorful hairpins, Shirin looked more like a big beautiful doll than a three-year-old child.

Only a hundred dollar bill and few singles remained of Mina's money. She had spent two hundred seventy dollars for the room and twenty dollars for the taxi. The driver had asked for twelve dollars; Mina gave him a twenty and told him to keep the rest. She had tipped the doorman a ten-dollar bill. He had opened the door for her and helped Shirin to get out of the taxi. Two hundred fifty dollars for a Jones of New York skirt suit, one hundred thirty dollars for Shirin's shiny black patent leather shoes and her own brown suede shoes. She had spent over an hour buying the finely detailed shoes with two-inch heels. She had seen the shoes in the window of

Nordstrom on her way to work. At first the salesperson could not find the shoes in Mina's size in the color she wanted. She had bought the suit in beige to match the brown color of the shoes. With the help of his supervisor, the sales clerk had retrieved the brown shoes in her size from the window display. Shirin's dress cost eighty-three dollars, her teddy bear thirty five.

They had changed in the restroom before lunch, and dumped their old clothes in the trashcan. Their lunch in the Nordstrom restaurant cost her fifty dollars. Mina ordered anything she thought Shirin might like; a big double cheeseburger; a plate of chicken wings; and an array of sodas, one of each color: Pepsi, Seven Up, and Fanta. She didn't care about them having too much sugar and being unhealthy. And for dessert she ordered a big bowl of ice cream, one scoop of each kind: vanilla, orange, strawberry, and chocolate. She herself only had a bite of Shirin's cheeseburger because she insisted. She did not feel hungry at all.

The waiter, a young girl, was as excited as Shirin. "You are a lucky little girl, having a mommy like her!" the waiter said to Shirin.

The smile disappeared from Mina's face. She felt guilty.

• • •

While paying for the room, Mina noticed the stores on the mezzanine. In a nail salon, an Asian girl was applying polish to a young woman's toenails. The woman's pants legs were rolled up to her knee. Another girl, who looked like the first one, sat behind one of the chairs, not doing anything. Mina went in and checked the prices. Twenty dollars for a pedicure and fifteen for a manicure. The third time Mina passed the store the girl who was not working called out to her and said something incomprehensible. She had a very thick Vietnamese accent.

The girl came out of the store: "You do yo nails, yo daughter free," she said in more understandable words.

Mina hesitated. She did not have enough money. She looked inside her wallet and counted the remaining money. She could only spend thirty dollars.

"Just our toenails," she told the girl. "I want it red. Both of us red."

After the pedicure was done, Mina gave her the money and tip, and went to her room. Shirin could not stop looking at the bright red color of her toenails.

The bathroom captured Mina's attention the most: a chrome shower behind a round glass door, and a Jacuzzi bathtub, with white towels, a white terry robe, and the same color slippers.

Although showered in the morning, she could not resist a hot bath. She turned on the TV for Shirin and returned to the bathroom and let the hot and cold water run while she poured the liquid soap in the water. A delightful aroma of lavender filled the room. She took off her clothes, pinned her hair up and covered it with a towel. She twisted the two ends of the towel up, the same way she had seen in the movies. The bathtub filled with a white foam. She rolled a towel and placed it on the edge of the tub, then lay down in the tub, rested her head and closed her eyes. The bathroom's radio played soft music.

By eight o'clock, she had dressed up and had her hair

set. She covered her face with the moisturizing lotion she found in front of the mirror, drew a narrow line above her eyelashes with an eyeliner, rouged her cheeks and colored her lips with lipstick. She examined her face in the mirror carefully. Her lips looked dull. She coated her lips with another layer of lipstick and rubbed her lips together to shine them, and spread the blush on her cheeks with the tip of her fingers. She didn't need mascara; her eyelashes were long and full enough. Her face looked glowing and the lines under her eyes disappeared. She looked ten years younger than the day before.

Mina rubbed a damp hand towel over Shirin's skirt and softened its wrinkles. She tossed the towel into the dirty linen basket, and with another towel cleaned the chocolate from her face. Shirin was too busy with the small shampoo and hair conditioner jars to complain.

Now they were ready for dinner. The last hundred-dollar bill was for dinner at the revolving restaurant on the top floor.

They held their hands together and left the room. To go to the top-level they had to descend to the ground level and get another elevator to the restaurant.

The first elevator's walls were made of glass. Shirin pressed her face to one glass and watched the concrete shaft moving in front of her eyes. When they got out of the tunnel and Shirin could see the empty space of the lobby, she let out a scream of joy and dread, and hid behind Mina's skirt. Mina hugged her, and together, they watched the sinking of the elevator into a small pond in the lobby. Tall, green tropical leaves swarmed the waterfall in the corner of the pond.

A hotel employee showed them the elevator that would take them to the restaurant on the thirty-fourth floor. The second elevator moved quickly to the top of the hotel without making a stop. Shirin shrieked with joy. They entered the restaurant hand-in-hand while laughing aloud.

The maître d', a courteous, young man with a mustache welcomed them, "This way, ladies." He led them to a table at the corner of the salon.

His expression looked familiar. "Your host, Marlin, will be with you shortly to take your order," he said politely, while drawing a chair from the side of the table for Shirin. He had a slight accent.

Marlin, tall, blonde and slim showed up shortly. She wore a mid-size black skirt, a trimmed white shirt, and a small bow tie around her neck, "Here is a coloring book and crayons for the sweet little lady and a menu for the mommy," she smiled. "What would you like to drink?"

Mina ordered a Coke for herself and a glass of orange juice for Shirin. Marlin came back with the drinks.

"We have five specials tonight," she said. Mina recognized none of them, except for one that was prepared with lamb shank.

"How do you cook your lamb shank?" Mina asked.

Marlin explained the process of marinating the lamb the day before with special spices, then serving it grilled, with asparagus sautéed in butter.

As she saw an approving smile on Mina's face, she said, "This one is my favorite. I really recommend it. It is our manager's special."

Mina ordered the lamb meal, and upon Marlin's recommendation, chicken breast with mashed potato for Shirin.

The dark-haired manager led two new customers to the next table; a young man in a dark gray suit and a woman in a blue tailored skirt suit. Mina could watch the manager from where she sat. Now his face looked familiar. Where had she seen him? Was he a customer of Mr. Kumar's? All Mr. Kumar's customers were Americans, except for some of his Indian friends and family. The man's face was Middle Eastern; he could even be an Iranian. Mina was sure she had seen him before. The expression in his eyes and his shy smile were familiar.

The young man regarded the woman respectfully and in a formal way. The woman picked up the wine list and studied it. The man watched her, quietly. She showed an item in the list to Marlin and asked her a question. Marlin brought her a bottle of red wine, poured a small amount in the crystal wine goblet in front of her, stepped back, and waited courteously. The woman gently swirled the glass back and forth. She then sniffed the wine and sipped a bit. She nodded her satisfaction. Smiling, Marlin poured the wine into both of their glasses and said she'd be back to take their orders for dinner.

Mina picked the wine list from the table and browsed through it. She didn't know the kind, or the brands of the wines. She had not had wine since she left Tehran. The prices went from fifty-four to nine dollars a glass. She calculated the bill in her mind and called to the server, "May I have a glass of chardonnay?"

"Great choice. Which one would you like to have?"

Mina glanced at the prices and said, "Kendall

Jackson."

"Excellent wine."

The price for a glass of Kindle Jackson was eleven dollars and with tax and tip, it would come to thirteen dollars fifty six cents.

The bill came out to eighty-three dollars. Mina left the hundred-dollar bill on the table and got up to leave. The maître d' came to her table. Mina stole a glance at his nametag pinned to his jacket.

"Hamid Pashaee, Manager."

Hamid! Hamid Pashaee? Was he the same Hamid? Sergeant Pashaee's nephew?

"Was everything okay ladies?" Hamid said, his accent disappearing now.

Yes, it was him for sure. "Oh yes, yes, everything was great." She grabbed Shirin and before he could recognize her, they swiftly left.

• • •

Shirin fell asleep in the second elevator. It was not easy to hold her; she would be four in three months.

The sky appeared behind the window as they entered the room. It was without a patch of clouds, moonlit and full of stars. On the corner of the bed, where the blanket and the bed sheets folded back, a note wished her sweet dreams, next to it a mint chocolate. Mina laid Shirin in the bed, picked up the note and the chocolate and went to the window. She had never seen Los Angeles's sky so beautiful; clear and bright, and without the layer of smog which usually concealed the stars. Now it looked like Borazjan's sky, the same translucent brightness.

How much she loved the nights they slept on the roof.
Mother placed Mahnaz and Mina's bedding next to her
own, and Hossein and Father's a little further. Mina and
Mahnaz stayed awake for some time after Mother went
to sleep and watched the sky and stars. They each chose
a bright star and followed its path across the sky. Mina
loved the moonlight. She would stay awake even after
Mahnaz went to sleep and read a book or watch the other
roofs and make up imaginary stories.

She unwrapped the chocolate and put it in her
mouth, then looked out the window. Downtown was
under her feet in its entirety. The neon lights on top of
the buildings winked at her. To the right was a new
building with dark glasses and to the left an old short
white one. She could even see signs of the ocean faraway
in the distance. How close the Pacific Ocean was to her
and at the same time how far! Why did she never go to
the beaches with Shirin? Shirin would've loved it. How
far was the Atlantic Ocean from her? How far was she
from all the seas and the oceans, and all the plains and
meadows and date palm orchards of the world? And
from the Caspian Sea and the Persian Gulf, and the Lut
desert?

Mina extended her arm out of the window and let go
of the crumpled up chocolate paper. The paper ball
plunged toward the street and disappeared from her
sight in a blink of an eye. Mina poked her head out and
stared down. The sidewalks looked far and frightening.
She shut the window rapidly. No, she should not rethink
it. She had made her decision, and nothing should
change it.

Mina retrieved her passport – the only identification

document she had – and went to the bathroom. She found an ashtray with a matchbox engraved with the hotel's logo next to the sink. She struck the match and held its yellow flame under the passport.

The passport's plastic cover warped, and the lion and sun logo had started to fade. Mina opened the other pages. She lit the first page, the page with the stamp of The Islamic Republic of Iran, and then the page with the American entry visa. The visa had expired long ago. She burned the other pages together. Then, she threw what was left of the passport into the toilet bowl and flushed.

The semi-burned cover spun on the water's surface, disappeared for a moment, but came back up with the new water in the bowl. Mina flushed the toilet again but the passport would not disappear. Using her hand, she dragged the passport out. There was no comprehensible text remaining on the passport cover, but its burgundy color could betray her. She dried it with one of the face towels, then put it in the sink, and again tried to burn it. After she had lit the last matchstick, the remainder of the passport was nothing but black ash.

She had given the receptionist her fake green card, with a wrong telephone number and address; now there was no way to identify her. The fake green card had been a gift from the recruiter who found her the job in Mr. Kumar's restaurant.

She looked at the clock. 10:30. She should wait until the streets grew empty.

She turned the television on and sat to watch the final part of a movie on the classic channel. A western she had seen in Tehran years ago. John Wayne played in it. His accent was unfamiliar. She had seen several of

John Wayne movies in Iran and liked his thick, heavy Persian patois. Now she couldn't understand a word he said!

When the movie ended, she glanced at the clock again. It was almost midnight.

She had avoided looking at Shirin's eyes directly since they entered the hotel. They both were very happy all day. Shirin had hugged Mina and kissed her many times. Mina looked at the bed. Shirin slept with one of the crayons still in her hand. Her beautiful pink dress was wrinkled and dirty. Mina took the teddy bear from the floor and left it next to Shirin. The white small teddy bear looked at the ceiling with its lifeless, button-like eyes.

Mina pushed a chair next to the wall by the window, opened it, and without glancing out went to the bed and picked Shirin up. She avoided looking at her face.

She held Shirin closer and using the chair, she sat down on the windowsill. Her tight skirt made it harder to lift up her legs. She pressed her back to the glass, closed her eyes, and tried to relax her mind. Did Hamid recognize her? He had changed a lot. Was he married now? Did he have any children?

She opened her eyes and looked at Shirin. Shirin slept serenely. Mina could not resist kissing her chick. Shirin opened her eyes and smiled. Her dimples deepened and the black of her eyes shone. "Mommy, mommy I love you." She lifted her hands and threw her arms around Mina's neck. Her breath smelled of strawberry, of chocolate, of vanilla; she smelled of all the sweetness in the world. Oh... how flattering her babyish voice was... mommy I love you... "I love you too my dear, my dearest. Mommy loves you..."

She got up from the ledge, came down from the chair quickly, and rushed to the bed. She tucked Shirin in and went back to close the window.

• • •

A week later, Mina sent a short note to Hamid. He came the next day. He had changed a lot, but he was as shy as she could remember him.

The second time, he brought toys and chocolate, and took Shirin to McDonald's. He was on a mission to rescue them both.

Los Angeles - Hamid

"Maman... Maman... come on... come on Maman...come here. Come listen to her, please, just one more time," Shirin called Mina while holding a doll. "Look how ticklish she is?" Her own laughter louder than the doll's.

The talking-doll was Hamid's gift to Shirin the night before. She played with the doll until midnight and took it to bed afterward. When she woke up, she started to play with it again, not paying attention to Mina's request to get ready for nursery. The doll had long platinum hair and shiny staring blue eyes. When Shirin touched any part of her body, she talked about that part loudly. Shirin wouldn't get tired of touching her belly. The doll would start to laugh and talk: "My belly is sensitive to your touch because...," then she would tell you about the other body parts that were sensitive to touch.

Mina grabbed the doll, put it aside, and started to tickle Shirin under her arms and her belly. "If you don't get ready I will tickle you until you pee your pants!"

Shirin laughed harder. Mina picked her up and took her to the shower.

Their apartment was now full of toys that uncle Hamid had brought Shirin in the past nine months.

Unlike uncle Hossein, who was not aware of having a niece, or if he were he ignored it completely, uncle Hamid came to see them twice a week. Shirin could not wait to see him. Each time, he made a date with Shirin for the next visit: A date to spend all day at Disneyland, Magic Mountains, Knott's Berry Farm, or dinner at McDonald or Burger King. If Mina had time, she would go with them; otherwise, Hamid took Shirin with him. He was like a brother Mina never had.

Hamid finally asked the question Mina expected:

"Where is your husband?"

"I got pregnant from a man I knew in Iran. No marriage involved," Mina simply responded.

For the first time they gazed at each other's eye. She finally had told someone. At least one person must accept her and Shirin the way they were. Hamid smiled shyly and lowered his eyes; a smile Mina liked in Hamid more than anything else.

Upon Hamid's insistence, and with the help of a lawyer customer he had, Mina applied for political asylum. In a short while she got her work permit, and financial aid for being a single mother.

Hamid had received his civil engineering degree from a university in the central US, and then had come to LA to find a job. However, the only job he had found was the assistant manager of the restaurant at the Bonaventure hotel. He had plenty of experience in this field as a student. Then he was promoted to the day shift manager and soon after to the night shift.

"I didn't want to be an engineer. I went to school for it just because my father wanted me to," said Hamid on few occasions. "I would love to have my own French restaurant somewhere far from downtown and develop it into a franchise one day."

Mina gave a quick bath to Shirin, dressed her, and they left home. She had to be at work at eight o'clock. Now she worked at an engineering firm as an intern from eight to one, and went to school four evenings a week, working on her MBA. She picked up Shirin from the nursery and spent time with her until three o'clock, she then took Shirin to the babysitter and went to school. The nights he was not working, Hamid offered to help. Then she stayed at school after her class and went to the library to study, or went to a coffee shop with Carlos, her classmate, to study and copy his notes, and laugh at his jokes.

Besides the difficulty of the classes, Mina had to spend some time every day looking up words in the dictionary. Studying with Carlos made it easier. Though Carlos was from Venezuela, he was fluent in English. He explained words to Mina when she did not understand them; in return, Mina tutored him in math and accounting. He had a heavy Portuguese accent pronouncing all Zs as S and all Vs as B. He was very handsome. A mix of European and indigenous people of Latin America; his eyes light, his skin dark, and his shoulder-length-brown hair curly. When he sat next to

163

Mina, her temperature went up. She tried hard to sit as far away from him as possible, and refused his daily invitations to have dinner or go to movies with him; her excuse was having to work hard or having to be with Shirin. Then if Carlos ignored her or studied with another female student, Mina got jealous and flirtatiously tried to get back his attention. A flirtation that continued throughout the two years of graduate school.

• • •

Mina left Shirin with Hamid early in the day and went to UCLA for the graduation ceremony.

Hamid and Shirin showed up right before the ceremony started. With a huge bunch of white and pink mums in his hand, Hamid stood out in the audience. He wore a gray suite with navy blue stripes, and a red, patterned tie. His short hair, short mustache, and well shaven beard made it obvious that he had just come from a barbershop. Shirin sat next to him, holding a big brown teddy bear and a bunch of tuberoses, Mina's favorites. She loved their smell. Hamid didn't overlook any detail.

As Mina's name was called from the speaker, Hamid rose, held Shirin up, and they both shouted: Bravo Mina ...Hurra Mina ...*Meena! ... Meena! ... Meena!...*

Hamid was tall and slender, with slightly scoped shoulders and a visible curve in his back; his hairline receded on both sides of his forehead. Mina waved to them.

They called Carlos to the platform right after Mina.

He pulled the black satin graduation cap from Mina's head, as he stood beside her. He threw it up in the air, and before it fell to the ground, he grabbed it and put it back on her head. He then pulled her closer and kissed her on her lips. Mina's eyes opened in wonder; this was the first time Carlos had kissed her. Her body warmed with hot flashes. She wanted to push him away, but her hands wouldn't follow her intentions. She peeped at Hamid and Shirin. They were not looking at them.

On the way down the platform, Carlos put his hand around Mina's shoulder: "You should come to Juan's party with me. He has invited all of my friends, and he specifically asked me to take you with me."

Mina glanced at Hamid and Shirin. They were waiting for her at the foot of the platform. As she reached down, they both rushed to her and gave her their flowers. Hamid took couple of pictures of Shirin and Mina with his camera. Carlos came to them and introduced himself: "I am Carlos, Mina's friend."

Mina's heart pounded frantically.

She introduced them, "My childhood friend, Hamid, and my darling daughter, Shirin." She added in a hurried voice, "Hamid's like a brother."

Hamid averted his eyes from Carlos and looked inquisitively straight into Mina's eyes. Mina lowered hers.

Carlos shook hands with them. "Do you want me to take a picture of you three?" Without waiting for an answer, he took the camera from Hamid and started to play with it. Not knowing what to do, Mina swiftly said, "Oh yes, yes, thanks."

"Closer, closer, put your hands over her shoulder.

She doesn't bite!" said Carlos with a theatrical pose.

Hamid blushed and smiled meekly, but he did not get closer to Mina. In all the pictures, Shirin stood between them and held their hands. Mina had not looked directly at the camera or at Carlos. With that square black cap, that long blue satin cape and the two large bouquets of flowers in her hand, she looked funny.

"Okeydokey, I get to go. I have a bery fun party to attend!" He winked at Mina. "Don't be late! Our friends are waiting."

Mina didn't answer. Hamid looked at Shirin intensely. Shirin went to Mina and held her hand: "Mom, we have a surprise for you!" Her eyes flashed with joy. Mina looked at Hamid. Hamid said he was taking them for dinner to celebrate her graduation.

They went directly to Hamid's place of work at the Hotel Bonaventure.

● ● ●

The gentle turning of the floor brought a new scene in front of their eyes every moment. Shirin stood next to the floor-to-ceiling window, and watched the buildings, totally amazed. Despite Hamid's numerous invitations, this was the first time Mina had returned to the restaurant; three years, two months and eight days. Shirin didn't seem to remember anything from that night but Mina could remember every minute. She had not told Hamid, or anyone else, why she was there that night. She tried hard to wipe off the memory. She hated that place.

After welcoming them, the evening manager led

them to a table next to the window where a bottle of Champagne in a bucket of ice was waiting for them. Jennifer was their server. Although she did not know them, Mina had heard about all of the restaurant's employees. Marilynn had married and left; Hamid had given Jennifer a raise recently; he had hired two new waiters: one with two years of experience, another one with five. Hamid told her all about his work. He was now the general manager. His work, food, Shirin, and occasionally Mina's education, were the only subjects they could communicate well about.

Hamid constantly talked about opening his own place. He even had found a partner, but they didn't have a proper location yet. After he traveled to Paris to get some ideas about what he wanted for his French restaurant, his plan was ready; the shape and size of the tables and chairs, the color and the design of the curtains, and the menu that was inspired by restaurants in the Champs Elyse. Twice a week, he went to different French restaurants and tried their food. If he liked a dish, he would ask the chef about the recipe. Then, at the first opportunity, he would invite Shirin and Mina to his apartment, cook the dish for them, and ask what they thought. He had recorded all the recipes in a thick notebook, marking their favorites.

Jennifer started to tell them about their specials, but as she named a dish, Hamid interrupted her, describing the ingredients and the way the dish was cooked. He recommended the roasted salmon with capers and mashed potatoes with garlic to Mina, and the hamburger with pineapple sauce to Shirin. He ordered lamb shank for himself. Mina looked at the clock; it was a quarter to six. She agreed with all his recommendations. Carlos had said she could come anytime she wanted. The party was supposed to continue until midnight.

Shirin, unable to sit still, got up two times and went to Hamid. Each time she whispered a few words into his ear and he whispered something back to her. Shirin smiled while looking at Mina. Mina only heard Hamid's words: "Later, with the dessert."

After the main dish, Jennifer, without asking them, brought the dessert. Hamid quietly watched Jennifer serving it. A tiramisu for Mina and a dish of strawberry ice cream for Shirin, and coffee for himself. Mina looked at Hamid. He smiled, blushing, lowering his eyes. Hamid knew Tiramisu was Mina's favorite dessert.

Shirin impatiently ate a few spoonful of her ice cream, then got up and went to Hamid. She touched his jacket's upper pocket and loudly said, "Uncle Hamid, what do you have in your pocket?"

"You can take it out and look at it if you want," said Hamid.

Their tone of voice, the way they looked at each other and the smiles they both tried to hide, reminded Mina of a play she and Maryam took part in in the elementary school. Every time they rehearsed the play, Maryam made Mina laugh so hard that they could not continue their lines. They lay down on the floor and laughed hysterically. On the day of the actual show, however, they performed so brilliantly that the next day Mrs. Tashakori gave them both special recognition. The recognition itself became another play for Maryam. She mocked it for a month, making everybody laugh.

Shirin pushed her hand inside Hamid's pocket and

took out a small giftwrapped box. She screamed dramatically, "A gift! Is this for me?"

Hamid blushed red and mumbled, "No. It is for your mom."

Shirin screamed with fake anger, "For my mom? Lucky her!" Then she came to Mina and handed the gift box to her. Hamid watched them enthusiastically. A small box wrapped in a golden paper. Mina looked at it hesitantly. "Open it," Shirin beseeched her.

Mina unwrapped the gift. A red velvet box appeared. She froze in her seat as she opened it; a platinum ring, with a large diamond in the middle and two smaller diamonds carved on each side, shone on a bed of white satin. "May I have the honor of marrying you?" was inscribed in gold on the satin.

Mina's eyes fixed on the ring for a moment, she then lifted her head and looked at Hamid inquisitively. Hamid blushed again. He looked like the teenage Hamid who had brought her the dead skewered sparrows.

Shirin leaned on Hamid and fixed her eyes on Mina. She seemed disappointed not seeing Mina jumping from her seat. Mina looked at the ring again. Shirin sat on Hamid's lap and Hamid wrapped his arms around her shoulder. A small bit of ice cream was dripping from Shirin's collar. Hamid took a white napkin from the table, dipped it in his glass of water, and wiped the spot. Shirin didn't pay attention to him, concentrating fully on Mina's reaction to the ring.

Mina's gaze moved back and forth between the ring and Shirin. Every time her eyes locked with Shirin's, Shirin smiled eagerly and pressed herself to Hamid.

She dropped her eyes down and said: "Yes," with a

trembling voice.

What else could she say? They looked like a happy father and daughter already.

Los Angeles - Marriage

<u>Nov. 1993</u>

8 large eggs

8 tablespoons fine white flour

8 tablespoons powdered sugar

100 grams heavy whipping cream – enough for use inside and outside the roll

4 tablespoons powdered sugar

A small amount of vanilla or lemon zest

Page five hundred seventy eight of the 20th edition of Roza Montazami's cookbook that Mother had sent her along with a rice cooker, a samovar and a beautiful Persian rug as her wedding gifts.

Mina placed a piece of aluminum foil in a baking sheet, greased the foil and sprinkled it with flour.

She turned on the oven and set it on 350 degree. Preheating the oven would help the bread to rise better.

She used two large bowls. In one, she added six egg whites and in the other, eight egg yolks; added 1.5 tablespoons sugar to the egg whites and used a mixer until the egg whites puffed up; added 4 tablespoons of sugar to the egg yolks, and blended them well. She then added the vanilla, the baking powder, the flour, and blended the mix again. It had been some time since she had learned how to add the flour without worrying about it not being dissolved properly into the mixture.

Next, she used a spatula to mix the contents of the two bowls gently. If she stirred the mixture too much, it lost its puffiness. She emptied the mixture into the baking sheet and spread it out evenly, then placed the sheet in the oven. After 15 minutes, she removed the cookie sheet from the oven, and put the foil over a wet towel. She mixed the heavy whipping cream with the remaining powdered sugar in another bowl until it became thick and formed a peak. She carefully put the mixture into the fridge. The bread separated from the foil without breaking. It came out in an even golden color. Satisfied, Mina smiled. Using a flat spatula she applied the whip cream to the inside of the bread and then gradually began rolling. Finally, she frosted the outside and both ends of the rolled bread.

According to the book, she now should grate some dark chocolate over the roulette, but Mina preferred to use her imagination. She decorated the roulette with several preserved sour cherries and dotted each with a half-pistachio nut. Then, she drew a couple of geometric lines around the sour cherries using the juice of the preserve. She placed the whole thing on a flat rectangle crystal dish that Khanum Bahadori, Hamid's aunt, had given her as a birthday gift. The roulette fit perfectly on the dish. She had been looking for a dish like that for a few months.

Mrs. Bahadori was very kind to Mina. She had done everything to fill up the vacant space of a mother-in-law for her; the empty space of *a poor sister, who had not seen any good of this world.*

For dinner, Mina had made *khoresht e fesenjoon* with steamed rice, *zereshk polo*, roasted chicken, meat roulette and barley soup. For appetizer, she had made shrimp cocktail with red sauce among many other Persian hors-d'oeuvres.

Everything was ready except for the rice. Cooking the rice wouldn't take more than fifteen minutes. She still had an hour and half before the guests arrived. She went to the bedroom, removed the rollers from her hair, and straightened each lock with care. As her hair got straighter, the golden highlighted streaks became shinier and more visible. She started to put makeup on. She moistened her face well with a cream, then covered the darker spots with a concealer, and finally covered her whole face with a liquid foundation and her eyelids with a brown shadow. She smeared white eye shadow under her eyebrows, and with a dark brown liquid eyeliner, she drew a thin line above her eyelashes. Would her *fesenjoon* come up ok this time? With a rather thick brush, she applied mascara to her longer eyelashes, then with a slimmer brush, she put mascara on the shorter, finer eyelashes on both sides of her eyes. Would Shirin and Hamid like the *fesenjoon* this time? She scanned her face in the mirror. Her eyes were ready. She put blush on her cheeks and on the two corners of her forehead and then dabbed her whole face with a layer of powder, the same color as her base foundation. She lined her lips with a dark cranberry color and smeared a lighter lipstick on her lips. No, it was still too dark. She placed a soft napkin between her lips and rubbed them together to remove the lipstick. She then coated her lips with a light purple color. She should go check on the food. She had tried hard to make everything the way they liked it. She had even checked with Mrs. Bahadori about the coarseness of the *fesenjoon's* walnut puree. She inspected her lips in the mirror again. It was much better now. She puffed perfume over the veins of her wrist and under her earlobes.

She was ready. She returned to the first floor to prepare the rice.

● ● ●

The swollen grains were ready to be cooked. She had soaked the basmati rice in a lukewarm water with plenty of salt, in the morning. She put a gallon of water in a pan and brought it to boil, then drained and added the soaked rice to the pot and added a tablespoon of rose water to it to enrich the aroma. The rose water was Mrs. Bahadori's idea. The cookbook said to boil the rice for 8 to 10 minutes and stir it to keep grains from sticking together. But she would do it for six minutes, precisely, and no stirring. From experience, she knew that the rice grains would expand more and become brighter if she took the rice out of the boiling water before it got too soft, and added some water after she had drained the rice and returned it to the pot to steam. When the mist rose from the pot, she would pour some hot melted butter over the rice. If the melted butter was not very hot, it left a greasy taste in the mouth.

In another bowl she mixed two tablespoons of yogurt, two egg yolks, ¾ cup butter, ½ cup water, a few drops of dissolved saffron water, and put it aside to later add it to the bottom of the pot before she added the rest of the rice. This helped making the *tah dig* golden and crispy. Hamid and Shirin loved her *tah dig*s. Strangely, they had the same taste in food, as well as in many other things. Sometimes Mina doubted whether they really shared the same taste in so many things, or they pretended to enjoy whatever the other one enjoyed just because they loved each other?

From where Mina stood, in front of the stove, she could see and hear the TV in the living room. A group of young girls and boys, their hair mostly bleached and spiked, danced hip-hop. The music suddenly stopped, and a stern looking newscaster showed up on the screen.

"The Islamic Republic News Agency of Iran a few minutes ago reported, 'The leader of the Islamic revolution and founder of the Islamic Republic of Iran, Imam Khomeini, passed away at a Tehran Hospital at 6 pm today.'"

The image of the dancers still danced on the background of the screen. The newscaster apologized for the pause in the program, and the sound of music returned.

Khomeini's dead!

For a second, Mina was motionless. Was that true? Was he really dead? One more page of history turned before her eyes! "What would happen now?"

She paced up and down the kitchen. The young soldier on top of the army tank with the fine mustache and the machinegun in his hand... the black-*chador* wearing women of the *Tasu'a* demonstration... Jaleh Square... Death to Shah, death to Shah... Molotov cocktail... Cocktail! Just like the shrimp cocktail with tomato sauce but in black...a color as black as *fesenjoon*! She had totally forgotten! The burner under the pot was too high. She turned the burner down, then looked into the pot. Oh no, the *fesenjoon* had not set yet! What would Khanum Bahadori say? Hamid certainly would smile one of his scornful smiles – the one Mina hated. Undoubtedly he would again insist that Mina should learn how to cook *fesenjoon* from his aunt. But Mina had worked hard this time to make sure her stew had simmered well and the oil had set the same way *Khanum* Bahadori's did. She had chopped the whole chicken and fried the pieces the way she did, finely grinded the walnut and added the same amount of pomegranate syrup as she did, and cooked it over a low heat for hours as she did. What a tedious task! She hated it. She always swore she would not cook it anymore, but *fesenjoon* was Hamid and Shirin's favorite stew. Every time they went to Khanum Bahadori's home, she cooked it for them. They never got tired of it. *Oh what a delicious khoresht! Oh how delicious it is! Its sweetness and tartness is just exact! Its oil is set exactly the way it should!* Mina changed the channel. How did Iran *Khanum* cook her fesenjoon? She was a good cook too. Had she finally learned to cope with her daughter's death? They had found Azar's dead body in the middle of Jaleh Square the day after Black Friday. She surfed the channels. Damn it! There were no more news! Did Bahram still support the Islamic Republic regime? What would have become of Mina if she had married him? If she could make her *fesenjoon* come out like Khanoom Bahadori's, then she could call herself a good cook! No, tonight she didn't want to be a good cook! Next time she would cook her *fesenjoon* anyway she wanted. She walked to the pantry and opened the door, couldn't remember why she did it and what she wanted, slammed the door and walked away. Aha! What a good idea. She would fry a skinless piece of chicken breast, she would cook the chopped walnuts and the pomegranate syrup separately, then she would cover the chicken breast with the sauce and let it simmer until it got the right taste. She might even use chicken wings instead of chicken breast. She would cook the wings in the pomegranate syrup, then spread sesame seeds over it and broil it in the oven. How about using almond instead of walnut? Or pomegranate seeds instead of the syrup? What difference would it make? Hamid would still not like it. He would glance at Shirin and smile, "Khanum Bahadori's stew is something else!" Fuck you and fuck Shirin! Fuck *khoresht fesenjoon*! Fuck Khanoom Bahadori! What does *fesenjoon* mean after all? Fe, sen, joon? If this time Hamid smiled his mischievous smile again, she would ask him, "Do you know what *fesenjoon* means at all?" She knew Hamid's response: "It means that greasy sweet and sour stew of my aunt;" and Shirin's comments: "Ooh *fesenjoon*!

What a great taste, I can feel its taste right now!" She would say it with that pimply, blemished face of hers, and those ugly metal braces on her teeth and that mischievous smile that she had learned from Hamid. *I can taste it right now!* You eat shit! Are you my daughter or *this* haughty, workaholic, over-eating man's? Does she even care that Mina married him just for her sake? She had totally forgotten that he was not her biological father. How can she forget? She was over six years old when they had married. Only seven years ago. One of these days Mina was going to tell her about that bastard, Mohsen. Had Mohsen's face, after he took the cyanide pills, turned pale or become dark purple like *fesenjoon*? Had his big body stayed motionless on the surface of the street or had he jerked to death? Did Khomeini like *fesenjoon*? How many times had *he* complained because Batool Khanum's *fesenjoon* had not set? What kind of *fesenjoon* had that peasant soldier liked? How about those women in black *chadors* who came to the demonstrations? Had they cooked *fesenjoon* for their husbands before they left home to make them happy? Or did they, like Mother, put the *aabgosht* pot on the stove before they left home? Oh...Was it six minutes yet? She looked at the clock. It was 7:20. When did she add the rice to the boiled water? She couldn't remember exactly. She took couple of grains of rice with a spoon from the pot and smashed them between her fingers. They were not soft enough. The day she went to the airport with the first ladies of the town to welcome Queen Farah, Mother first put the *aabgosht* on the stove, turned the burner down and left home. It was a dish that did not require much effort to make. Why that wasn't Hamid's favorite?

And Hamid's mother? How many times had she made *fesenjoon* for the honorable Major Colonel Pashaee? Perhaps if her stew had set like her sister's, the honorable Major Colonel would have not killed her so easily and swiftly! Perhaps on that afternoon, while she waited for her lover to show up, she had put the *aabgosht* on the stove to cook, so she could have more time to get ready for a passionate lovemaking. What did she have on her mind that day? Was she thinking, "After all these years of marriage and after having a child, finally I have found someone to give me sexual pleasure?" Had the honorable Major Colonel ever gave her an orgasm? Or Mr. Colonel, like Mohsen, only thought of his own pleasure? Or perhaps, like Hamid, he was so inexperienced and so naive that even with his good intentions, he did not know how to please a woman?

When Mina returned to the present, the rice had gone too soft and was completely ruined.

• • •

It was past twelve when the guests finally left. Mina spent two hours cleaning the dishes, sweeping and mopping the kitchen and cleaning the counters until they were shining. She could vacuum the family room the next day. Before turning out the light, she grind some coffee, poured it in the coffee maker with two big glasses of water, and adjusted its automatic clock for 7 am. Hamid liked the smell of fresh coffee. Mina took a tired look at the kitchen and the living room and smiled faintly; everything was in place. It was even cleaner and tidier than Mother's kitchen.

Hamid was asleep. While changing to her nightgown, Mina looked at her body in the mirror. She seemed chubbier. Her breasts were plumper and, although she was now in her late thirties, she looked younger. As Khanum Bohadori said: her skin looked juicier, her bones stronger. Her hair looked brighter under the direct light of the bathroom lamp. She turned and looked at her profile and run her finger over the arch of her nose. She then brushed her teeth and washed her face, but did not apply her night cream and eye cream as usual. She looked at herself again in the mirror. Her face looked very different without makeup.

She went back downstairs. She wished she had the strength to vacuum the family room right then, but these days she got tired faster. She covered the family room's Louis XVI style chairs and sofas with a white slipcover. They looked as ugly as ever. Why didn't she send them back when Hamid bought them without consulting her? She had only shrugged. Whatever. Why should it make any difference?

She stopped at Shirin's room, the only bedroom downstairs. Everything was clean and neat. Shirin did it herself. She had become as obsessed with cleaning as Hamid. Hamid was a great father and could be considered a good husband in many regards. If Mina needed anything, especially if it was for their home, he wouldn't blink an eye before buying it for her. He took them for long vacations two or three times a year. He loved to surprise them by announcing the place of the vacation. He had even shocked Mina about the new house. The house was far from the center of the city where Mina had always lived. A big four-bedroom house, located on the hillside of Woodland Hills, with a full view of the city. They could see the streetlights from their back yard and the master bedroom.

Mina tiptoed to the sliding door on the other side of Shirin's room. Shirin never fully closed the vertical blinds. She loved to watch the blue of the swimming pool and the Jacuzzi, while lying in her bed. This room had the best view in the whole house, although the torn up lawn and the BBQ and fireplace construction in the back yard obscured some of it now.

Shirin opened her eyes and jolted as she saw Mina standing there, "Oh... Mom! You scared me! What're you doing here?"

For a moment, Mina felt angry, but she controlled her feelings and kissed Shirin's face, "Sorry, sorry. I just came to kiss you before I go to bed," and left the room.

• • •

Hamid turned to his side, hugged Mina from behind, and put his right hand on her stomach. Mina quickly removed his hand and turned toward him. She should be careful.

Mina had received the lab result a week ago; she was a month and a half pregnant. She didn't talked about it with anyone; not with Hamid, who badly wanted another child, and not with Khanum Bahadori, who asked her every day if she was pregnant yet. Hamid always said "another child." He had legally adopted Shirin, had given her his name, and felt fully responsible toward her. He took her to piano lessons and dance class three days a week. He took Shirin to school in the morning, and Mina on her way back from work, picked her up. Shirin was thirteen now and Hamid wanted another child. Shirin, too, talked about having a little brother. "A man's head should always be busy with a kid," Khanum Bahadori encouraged her all the time. "Now that Hamid is *masha-allah* financially doing so well, I am sure lots of women have their eyes on him." "His body is perfect. He inherited his father's tall height and his mother's black bright eyes." She always sighed deeply when she talked about Hamid's mother, and sadly said, "God forgive her."

The baby could be a boy, a small, sweet-smelling baby boy. She could spend as much time as she wanted with him. She could feed him and give him life with the milk that streamed from her body. Something she had not had a chance to do for Shirin. She wouldn't have to leave him with a babysitter all day and go to work. She could dress him with whatever clothes she wanted, could put him in a baby stroller and go to the park or shopping. She could take him to school every day and see him finding friends, falling in love and becoming a man. Perhaps, finally, she could begin to know men better. Hamid was nice and kind, but... How little had she seen and known Mohsen? How about Parviz? If he had a normal life and had not been tortured to death, what kind of husband and father would he be? She even never knew Hossein well and never felt close to him. When they were kids, he always wanted to order her and Mahnaz around and play the role of a big overly protective brother, and later, when Mina needed him the most, he fully disengaged himself from her and her life.

He only began to have a relationship with Mina after she married Hamid. For sure he was grateful to Hamid for saving his disgraceful sister! Mother had chosen Hossein's wife for him in Iran and had sent her to Turkey for him to pick up. He went there for a week and met her for the first time. Now they had a son and a daughter who loved their auntie Mina and uncle Hamid dearly.

Did she really want another child? Despite having a full time job, she also maintained to be a real, completely engaged housewife. She had become the low-grade petite bourgeois she always dreaded of becoming. What had happened to her dreams? All those talks and discussions she had with her friends, hopes she shared with them? What happened to all those books she wanted to read and all those movies she wanted to watch? Working all day and taking care of the never-ending household chores did not leave her any time or energy. She used to read for a while in bed before falling asleep, but now she could only keep awake to read a page or two. Hamid was not into politics and "those kinds of foolish games," and "intellectual show offs." He never liked to see a movie unless it was an old Western or a cheap comedy. He said he worked seventy to eighty hours a week and needed his peace of mind and quietness when he came home. He had made his family life the way he had always dreamed of. He had bought a white S500 Mercedes Benz for his wife and a black Cadillac for himself. He exchanged their cars with newer models every few years. He loved his wife and his daughter and had good friends and relatives to enjoy; Khanum Bahadori, her son and daughter in law, who was jealous of Mina's relationship with Khanum

Bahadori; Hossein and his wife and his two children who were Mina's only relatives in America; Hamid's business partner, his wife and three sons. Mina despised all these, but Shirin loved it all. Did she remember the old lonely miserable life with Mina and their hostile neighbors? Did she remember the time Mina almost took her life, the life of her own child? How much more she needed to sacrifice to earn Shirin's forgiveness?

Mina turned and faced the other side of the bed. Four people could easily fit in that large bed. The bedroom was as big as Mina's old apartment. She missed her apartment; that apartment with all its books and posters she had hung from the walls and doors, and her small black and white decrepit television, and that big money tree plant she had rescued from Mr. Kumar's restaurant. All those things that had *belonged to her*. How much had she hated that room and all its stuffs those days! Now she missed them all. She had stored the books in four boxes along with an old suitcase in the spare room. Once in a while she bought a new book, read it, and then stored it in a box next to the other books. What was wrong with her? What did she want? What did she expect of life? Wasn't it enough that she did not have financial insecurities, had a big comfortable house, a happy successful daughter, a little baby on the way, and friends and family to spend time with, chatting about food, weather, the trips they had taken, their houses and cars? She did not have to worry about Shirin's future anymore. Was life anything beyond these simple joys? Why did she always look down at Hamid for all these? Hamid had worked hard enough to arrange this comfortable life for her and Shirin, and many more kids if they wanted. Mother was happy too. Now Mina could call and talk to her as much as she wanted. Mahnaz lived in Sweden as a political refugee. She badly wanted to publish her poetry book but didn't have money. Mina could send her some money. She even didn't have to tell Hamid about it. But no, she could not lie to him. Although he had never complained about whatever money Mina spent, he would still want to know how it was used. He would not object to sending money to Mahnaz, but Mina hated explaining everything to him.

Recently Hamid had begun to suggest that Mina should quit her job and stay home to take care of the family. Perhaps he hoped she could learn how to make *fesenjoon* as well as Mrs. Bahadori! Great, she could finally see that pleased look on Shirin's and Hamid's faces. How about her son? Would he like *fesenjoon* as much as Hamid and Shirin? What would be his name? Should she name him Parviz?

• • •

Mina got up at 4 am, went to the first floor and turned on the TV. She turned down the sound and switched the channel to CNN. She was right; CNN showed Khomeini's funeral ceremony. It was a rerun of an earlier live program.

The camera showed Khomeini's open coffin placed on top of a green Range Rover. The car was similar to the one that had taken him to Behesht e Zahra cemetery the first day he arrived in Tehran, the day Mina, and many other people, ran along it in the streets.

Loud *"Allah o Akbar"* chanting filled the street. The

car could hardly move through the crowd. A group of people climbed up to the top of the car, to the coffin, and tried to tear up pieces of the shroud and take them for blessing. The white shroud was pulled in every direction. For a few seconds, she saw Khomeini's corpse. His eyes were closed under his dense black eyebrows, his naked legs slender and colorless, his turned-to-blue toenails long. The camera stopped on the corpse for a moment, then turned to the masses. Many people wept and harshly stroked their heads and chests.

What would happen in Iran now? Was there any chance of radical changes? If the leftists came to power, there would be many social changes. She could go back and put her life back in order. She could take Shirin with her and live the way she wanted. Shirin now had an official father. She had the right to live!

Mina just needed to contact her old friends; the Student Supporters of the Democratic Movement in Iran and get some information. Were they still operating? Most of them were not students anymore. Probably now, many of them, like her, had their own families, jobs, luxury homes and cars. Did any of them still dream of going back? How long had it been since she talked to Parvaneh? Her old friend from the Khaneh e Iran. Nine years? Ten years?

• • •

A few days later, Mina called Parvaneh. She had to look for her number all over. She finally found it in an old address book she had tossed in a suitcase where she kept all her old memories. Luckily, the number had not changed.

"Salaam Parvaneh. This is Mina, do you remember me?"

"Mina? Which Mina?"

"Mina Sha'abani. We saw each other last in Khaneh e Iran."

"Oh, yeah. Salaam, how are you? How is your daughter? You came with her. She was so sweet."

"Yes, yes, Shirin. She is fine, she a teenager now."

"Actually about five years ago I was looking for you all over, but nobody had any clue where you were. Someone who knew you from Iran was looking for you. Her name is Zary. I remembered you were asking if anyone Knew her in Iran."

"Oh...Yes, Zary! Is she still here? Do you have a number for her?" Mina couldn't be happier. Zary? Oh my God! Zary's here!

"I haven't seen her in the past couple of years. I don't have any number for her, but I know she befriended some of the Sandinistas supporters. I think they still have their meetings at the same place downtown. You might be able to find her there."

I can't believe it! Oh my God, she has been here all this time and I did not know!

Mina found Zary in the House of Nicaragua, where she formerly knew as Khaneh e Iran. No sign of any Iranian activities there. All posters and banners were gone. Everything was about Sandinistas and their upcoming election. A big banner hung on the wall.

"The People United Will Never Be Defeated."

"El pueblo unido jamás será vencido."

With her small body, short dark hair, casual khaki pants, and an olive green military jacket, Zary could be easily mistaken for a Latin American young boy. Buttons were pinned all over her jacket: A bright red "Peace" button next to a purple "Pro Choice" on its lapel; "No war," "My Body My Choice," "International unity," "Amnesty International," "Peace on Earth," "We support our troops, bring them home alive," "War is not pro-life", and other pins decorated her chest. Mina liked this one the most: "Wars Undo Mothers' Work." Her heart grieved for Maryam Aliabadi when she saw it.

After thirteen years they had found each other again. Mina never thought she would see Zary in Los Angeles. She hadn't even been sure Zary was still alive. She assumed she was in prison or, like so many others, executed. It had been many years since Mina stopped searching for her. She had not even been following the news on the political situation of Iran or the world. She had lost many people she had known, including the ambitious Mina she knew before.

After that first time, they met again several times and Zary updated her on the news. Sometimes Zary wore a Che Guevara beret with a pin showing the same picture of Che that Mina had seen the first time in the Siahkal's memorial in Tehran. Another time she wrapped around her neck a black and white Palestinian keffiyeh, with both ends knitted with the color of the Palestinian flag; red, black, white and green.

What would Khanum Bahadori say if she saw Zary? "Oh no, God save us! What is this getup this girl has made for herself? She looks like a clown! I can't believe it! You and your friends Mina joon!" she would remark and then wink to Mina to show they were still on good terms. But Khanum Bahadori would definitely not understand much about Zary's ordeals in Iran, the things that had happened to her and how she had escaped death in prison.

Mina's Revolution

Tehran - Evin Prison

<u>Jan. 1983 / Azar 1366</u>

Name: Zary Ahmadi – a member of the traitor group OIPFG
Crime: Distribution of May 1st commemoration flyers and conspiracy against the Islamic Republic
Sentence: Ten years in prison
Prison: Evin

Zary couldn't believe it when they handed her the temporary release permit. It *must be a prank!* She thought. There was still five years left of her sentence. They must be taking her for execution, just as they took Kobra and Sepideh and Afkham and Ester and Zahra and Azar and Pari and Zohreh and Sima and Parichehr and Elham and Helena and Fariba and Farkhondeh and Farzanhe and Salime and Sedigheh and Sara and Soghra and Saeedeh and Fatimeh and Mahboobeh and Mah Lagha and Khadijeh and Faranak and Belghais and Helga and Parvin and Ronal and Farideh, and...

No, it was true. They had given her a week off to go home. Her father was dying and she could go home to spend a week with him. She could see him at least one more time! She could also visit Narges! She missed them both a lot. It was one year since Zary saw her father, and they had separated Narges from her about three weeks ago.

She had thought her father was dead, during the past year. He had stopped coming to visit her long ago; right after they killed Ahmad, Zary's younger brother. Ahmad was a supporter of the Mujahedin. He was killed on a street fight. Passdaran had followed him through several streets and shot him as he tried to get away by jumping on a rooftop. The death of the older brother, Reza, had not had the same severe effect on her father. Reza was arrested for collaboration with the Kurdistan's independence supporters, the Peshmerga guerrillas. The Islamic Republic hung him right after a brief trial. He did not have a lawyer and no one was in the court with him.

"He is too old, coming all the way to Evin would make him tired," her mother said if Zary asked about her father. "He is not well. He sent his regards to you," or "He can't stand seeing you behind the bars."

Zary couldn't believe her. Father loved her more than that. He wouldn't miss any occasion to see her. For sure, he had passed away. He must have died of grief, of the pain of losing two sons, the sons he loved so much. He must have believed that Zary would be executed or die under torture too.

She had even mourned for him, crying silently while she slept on the old soiled blanket, which was both her cover and her mattress, next to Ester and Simin. They moaned and groaned all night from the agony caused by the long tortures they both endured during the day. The prison cell was so small that if someone who was resting her back against the wall stood up, several people rushed to sit at her place to rest their backs. On one double bunk bed which was made to sleep one person, slept ten, and sometimes twelve. They made two long ropes from the old clothes and bed sheets and stretched them in front of each bed so that ten of them could sleep widthwise on the bed, and relax their feet on the rope. In the remaining space of the cell, one by two meters, lay the ones who were tortured and lashed in the past few days. Their pained sobbing took sleep away from others.

The inmates thought Zary's tears were from the pain of the infected flash on her back, or the pain of her blackened inflated right toe, which she could not fit in her shoe anymore. The guards had whipped her back and tore up the soles of her feet until she became unconscious, every day during the first month of her arrest, and then anytime they thought they could get some secret information out of her.

Her tears were for the wounds too, but missing her father caused her as much pain. Then she learned how to deal with the pain; not that she could make it disappear, she just made herself feel less pain. She learned how to meditate. Fatemeh, Narges's mother taught her how to do it.

Passdaran arrested Fatemeh and her husband

together, but they killed her husband right in front of her eyes. Narges was born in the prison. Everybody helped to take care of Narges, feeding her and washing her diapers, especially when they took Fatemeh for interrogation and she came back with a distorted body. However, it was Zary whom Narges loved the most; Zary was a second mother to her. Some nights, Narges slept all night with her. Zary, along with Fatemeh, taught her how to talk and walk.

Fatemeh sat in one side of the cell and Zary on the other side, while the other girls stood around. Fatemeh loosened her hold on Narges and Zary called on her as the others watched enthusiastically and encouraged her.

"Come, come to auntie, come my dear one, one more step, just one more, aha… you are almost here, bravo!"

Narges staggered, walked a few steps, and then fell. The day she walked all the way, and threw herself on Zary's lap was Zary's happiest day in the prison. The girls clapped and kissed each other with joy.

Then, one day they called Fatemeh to the office. Everybody tried to avert her eyes. She handed Narges to Zary, along with her will and two letters, one for her mother and one for her sister. She kissed all the girls in the cell and left. She never came back. Fatemeh's mother claimed Narges in a week.

One day the guards took Zary to the "Graveyard", because she did not wake up on time for the Morning Prayer, and then argued with the warden. Now Zary understood why they called that place a graveyard. Many people who went there never returned. She knew just two people who came back, and it took couple of months before they were able to talk or say anything making sense.

On the way, they fastened her eyes with a black rag. From the shortness of the way, she guessed they were taking her to the same area where the other wards were. When they got there, for a short second she moved her eye band away and peeped. There were many boxes against the walls. The boxes were made of wide pieces of wood and looked like above-the-ground, open-top, graves.

She shared one of the boxes with another prisoner. During the day, they had to sit inside the boxes, back to back, facing the prison walls, only twenty centimeters away. She had to sit there motionless, wearing a headscarf, a chador, and a pair of thick black stockings. They did not even allow her to move her head. She did not have any choice but to gaze at the wall all day long. A television droned on with prayers. After lunch, they let her lie down for about two hours. She slept in the same place after dinner. If she needed to use the bathroom, Sabieh, one of the Tawabs, the Repentant, who worked there, or one of the guards held her hand and took her to the bathroom. Nobody was allowed to talk to her, not even the Tawabs or the guards, except when they shouted at her or told her if she moved they would add days to her sentence.

Unlike others, Sabieh was kind. When nobody else was around, she talked to Zary. The first time Zary heard her voice her tears started running; Sabieh's voice was not the same as others. She did not shout at her or called her a slut. Her voice was soft and kind, the voice of a teenager, though not as cheerful as a sixteen year old's. She wiped Zary's tears with the corner of her chador, stroked her hair, and told her that she looked like her mother.

One day, after three weeks, when Zary was sitting in her grave someone took her to Hajj Davood, the prison's supervisor. He had news for her. Her Uncle, Hajj Abdullah, was taking her home for a short release.

• • •

Hajj Amoo Abdullah, Zary's oldest uncle, waited for her on the corner of Vanak Square in front of the old amusement park. The two guards in the prison's bus released Zary to him.

Hajj Abdullah had an old friendship with Hajj Davoud, the Evin's notorious superintendent. Uncle Abdullah was a prominent businessman in the Bazaar, importing and selling faucets. Hajj Davoud, used to be an important broker of metal. They had worked together for a long time.

Zary had not seen Hajj Amoo for more than ten years. His short beard had grown as white as his collarless shirt. He constantly counted his rosary beads with his fingers, avoiding looking at Zary. Zary's face was almost fully covered under a black scarf and chador.

"If your father dies, it's all your fault," Hajj Amoo said in Turkish, which Zary understood with difficulty. "Your poor mother is so embarrassed she could not look straight in anybody's face."

Hajj Amoo, as if he had thought of something, raised his head and gazed at Zary's eyes for a moment. Zary could not understand most of his words. Zary's father side of family was from Zanjan in the northwest, and spoke mainly Turkish. Father spoke Turkish with his relatives and Farsi with his wife and children. Zary's mother and children had learned some Turkish words in order to be able to talk to their grandmother and the older aunts. Hajj Amoo repeated his words in Farsi, and continued to speak with an accent that had made Zary smile in the past.

"This is the consequence of letting children be free to do whatever they want."

"How many times I told him 'Man! Be careful, look closer, watch what these kids are doing!' Those two were wasted like *that* and you turned out to be *this*!"

Zary's father was eight years younger than Hajj Amoo, and the first person in the family with a university education and an office job. He was so loved among his colleagues that after the Revolution, they voted for him to be the director; but he soon resigned and stayed home.

Doctors had lost hope in Father and had released him from hospital to go home and die among his loved ones. Colon cancer had spread all over his body. Zary's mother had begged Hajj Amoo's wife to ask him to appeal to Hajj Davoud to release Zary from prison for a few days to see her father. Mother was sure he would suffer and would not die until he saw Zary, his favorite child. Hajj Amoo's wife, a nice, sensitive woman, despite not liking Zary's mother much, asked Amoo to appeal to Hajj Davoud for God's sake.

Father died just two days after Zary came home. Mother was right. He was waiting for Zary. While he was alive, Zary sat by his side the whole time and held his bony hands, or wept while feeding him a light soup. He looked like a skeleton with a mouth and two sunken eyes.

The day her father died, all the relatives came to see them, many of whom Zary had never seen even before she went to prison. Mojtaba, Hajj Amoo's youngest son, Ahmad's and Zary's lovely childhood friend, who was Ahmad's age, and two years younger than Zary also came. He was now married and had three energetic sons.

Before the Revolution, Zary brought home leaflets of various political groups, which Mojtaba and Ahmad distributed among the neighborhood youngsters. The leaflets of Ayatollah Taleghani, a moderate clergy opposing the Shah, along with the political flyers of the Organization of the Iranian People's Fadaees and People's Mujahedin of Iran. After the Revolution, Ahmad joined the Mujahedin and Mojtaba became pro-Khomeini, and pressed by his parents, married their other cousin.

When Zary went to the kitchen to bring tea for guests, Mojtaba followed her. There was no one else in the kitchen. Mojtaba reached her and whispered to her: "Aghe Istah san man sanin, Ghachmaghini dooz al dah ram," Zary looked at him surprisingly. Mojtaba repeated his words in Farsi. "If you want, I can help you escape." Zary, nodded yes in disbelief. Mojtaba took the tray of the teacups and took them to the side of the family room where the men sat.

The next day, Mojtaba came back with more details.

• • •

On the afternoon of the third day of Father's death, the house was crowded. Friends and family came for the 3rd day commemoration. Hajj Amoo was to take Zary back to the prison the next day.

Zary could not sit quietly. She checked the clock every fifteen minutes. Ten minutes before six, Zary looked around. Her mother was crying silently in a corner. Pary, Zary's older sister, held her son in her arms and talked to one of the aunts and her daughter. Other people were engaged in talking as well. Zary went to her mother, and sat next to her, embracing her. Mother's cry became louder. For the first time since her father's death, Zary started crying too. After Mother's sobbing became quiet, Zary brought her mouth to her ear and whispered, "Please forgive me, I have to go."

Mother raised her head and looked at her. Where? To the prison? Zary stared at her. No...no. Not there. I am not going there even if I get killed. Don't worry. Just trust me. Mother looked at her, soundless, and with an intent gaze unfamiliar to Zary.

Before she left the room, Zary turned her head and looked at Mother for the last time. Mother was still watching her. Zary stared at her. What are you waiting for? I just need your approval, please don't deny me this. It might be the last request I have ever had of you. Mother nodded. Zary turned and left. She was sure Mother had blessed her departure. She knew Mother well. She knew she could always trust her and her infinite love. Mother was the one who had introduced her to books. Mother's education was limited to elementary school, but she had read many of the classical poems. When Zary was a small girl, instead of singing lullabies, mother recited Rumi's spiritual poetry and Baba Tahir's verses to her.

Downstairs, Zary entered the restroom, put on a heavy overcoat that Mojtaba had left there and changed her shoes and chador. Lowering the top of her chador to under her eyebrows, she swirled a corner of the chador around one hand and covered her mouth and part of her face with it. She looked in the mirror. No one would recognize this "Black Crow!" She was not even recognizable as a woman; a woman with big breasts, a curved waist, and prominent hips, a woman who could be sexy and desirable.

She opened the restroom's door and looked outside. Several other women in chador descended the stairs. Her eyes followed them. As soon as they got to the exit door, Zary got out of the restroom, reached the women, and left the house with them.

• • •

Mojtaba waited for her a few streets away in his car. His wife and three children, along with Hajj Amoo and Hajj Amoo's wife, were still at Zary's house.

Mojtaba took her to his apartment. He shaved all her hair and gave her a torn sheet to wind around her torso to hide her breasts, an oversized pair of boy's pants, and jacket to wear. Mojtaba smiled sadly, as he saw her in that outfit. Zary looked at herself in the mirror. She turned to Mojtaba and they both uttered, "Ahmad." She looked like a sixteen years old Ahmad. Zary's three weeks stay in the "Grave" had helped her lose most of her body curves.

An hour later, in the airport, Mojtaba introduced Zary to a middle-aged frail man who was to hand her to a Pakistani smuggler. After Mojtaba left, the man introduced Zary to a couple who were supposed to play her parents. He gave them their passports and put them on a plane to Zahedan.

It took five hours to get to Zahedan. A bearded man waited for them in the airport. He had an accent Zary could hardy understand. The man took them to the bus stop and together they traveled to Zabol. He told them he would take them to Kuwaiteh, at the border of Pakistan and Afghanistan, and there, someone else would receive them and inform them of their final destination.

Ahmad. Ahmad... AHMAD! They had to call her at least three times before she realized they were calling her. Ahmad? Which Ahmad? Her brother had been dead for years! He had died before she could see him one last time; before she could hug his head, which had lain on the curb, bleeding profusely, and say goodbye to him. No, Ahmad was not there, or maybe he was, maybe it was he who was going abroad to live his un-lived life. He was going somewhere else to continue the life he was deprived of.

She was Zary. But Nobody knew Zary. Which Zary anyhow? The energetic, cheerful Zary who was full of life and was arrested because she was defending freedom? Or that depressed, low-spirited, tortured girl that was handed to Hajj Amoo in front of the amusement park? Or that Zary who had sat in that one-by-half-meter grave and let her spirit fly out of prison and settle on top of the maple trees in Pahlavi street, the trees she had loved so much, and look down at the black crows walking under the trees? No, now she was none of them. Now, she was Ahmad. Zary did not exist anymore. She was the sixteen-year-old Ahmad. And how hard it was to be Ahmad, when, at the sign of any Passdar, her hand automatically went to the top of her head to bring down the edge of the chador she was not wearing anymore.

All the way, on the plane, in the bus, when they were walking on the mountains or the canyons, on the back of a horse or a mule – where she constantly felt she was on the verge of falling down – and again on the plane, she had tried hard not to think about her life in Tehran or in the prison, and about what would happen to her mother or to Hajj Amoo and what the government would do to them. Instead, she tried to make herself believe that she was Ahmad and he was traveling with his parents, Ali and Ashraf Hasanzadeh, speaking as little as possible so that others would not notice his soft feminine voice.

Los Angles - Zary

July 1994

Zary and Shirin became intimate from the first meeting. Shirin asked her, "Auntie Zary why is your left foot missing a toe?" With a stern gaze at Zary, Mina hinted that she didn't want Shirin to know.

It seemed Shirin had an extraordinary gift for becoming close to people from Mina's past; first Hamid and now Zary.

At thirteen, Shirin was as tall as Mina and Zary, but with larger bones. She had a round face, dark complexion, braces, and unlike Mina, straight smooth hair. Whenever Shirin's two deep dimples appeared on her face, Mina wished she could get rid of them with a plastic surgery. With those dimples, how could she forget Mohsen?

Zary never mentioned the resemblance between Shirin and Mohsen. Had she noticed? Did she know what had been going on between Mina and Mohsen? Mina should tell her one day. But with all the trust and respect Zary still had for Mohsen, would she believe her? Perhaps she should never tell her. What was the advantage of opening an old wound?

Zary was a vigorous pro-choice activist. Were they meant to meet again in this stage of Mina's life? Although Mina was never superstitious or even spiritual, she chose to believe it was a sign for her to make her mind about the baby she was carrying.

She asked Zary for help. Zary knew a doctor who worked in a Planned Parenthood clinic and made an appointment for Mina.

• • •

Both sides of the street were jammed with people, some watching, some shouting; all waiting for something to happen.

Mina had seen three police cars parked at the beginning of the street. As she got closer to the clinic, she saw the police standing here and there. It was most crowded in front of the building. How long was it since she had seen these kinds of scenes? Fourteen years? Fifteen?

A group of people, some with speakers in their hands, stood on one side, stopping the women from entering the abortion clinic. On the other side, the abortion supporters escorted women inside. The spectators, mostly business owners and their customers stood farther away on both sides.

Mina got closer to the clinic but wavered as she saw the TV cameras. A reporter from a local news channel was interviewing people both for and against.

There were pictures of fetuses, some fully formed with all the features of a child, next to them images of similar fetuses, all torn up and hideously dismembered. A number of men and women, holding Bibles and lifting up their placards, formed a circle behind the reporter.

Rescue those being led away to death; hold back those staggering toward slaughter

Know that the LORD is God. It is he, who made us, and we are his; we are his people, the sheep of his pasture (Psalm 100:3).

A man - or a woman - wearing a long black cape with a mask covering his face, approached Mina; his eyes sockets empty, his long boney yellow teeth poked out from his mouth. He held in his hand a plastic dead baby with no hands and feet. As he reached Mina, he shook the doll in her face and shouted, "Your child! Your child! I want your child!"

The doll's face looked like Shirin's. Mina stepped back and turned to leave.

"Mina, Mina!"

She turned back. Zary stood in front of the clinic. Mina walked toward her. As Mina got closer, people surrounded her . A few police officers chained their arms to stop the abortion protesters from getting closer to her.

The angel of death shook the doll at her face again. Someone from within the crowd shouted:

"Murderer!"

The Bible-holding group pushed the police chain and screamed at her: "For God's sake, don't do this Satanic act, for God's sake don't do it!"

"You shall not murder. "

"Hooray, hooray!"

"Go, go, go on. Don't stop!"

One supporter brought her flag closer to Mina's face. It was an image of a hanger crossed with red ink. She did not know what it meant. Zary waved her. As they reached each other, the line of the opponents broke the police line and rushed toward them. Zary put her arms around Mina and they ran to the clinic. The mob followed them to the door, but before they could get in, the guards closed the door behind Zary and Mina. They could still hear the angry cries from behind the closed door. Shortly after, a loud sound of shooting pulled them back to a window opening on to the street. One of the guards, the older, white one, lay on the sidewalk in front of the clinic. Blood streamed next to him on the asphalt. Everybody had fallen silent.

Mina panicked and started trembling. Zary held her in her arms, took her to one of the rooms, and lay her down in a bed.

● ● ●

The abortion procedure did not take longer than an hour. Then they put her in a recovery room for couple of hours until she woke up.

Zary held Mina's hand and caressed her hair. What a beautiful kind smile she had! Although her face was not as youthful as Mina remembered, her big brown eyes had the same vividness and glow.

A small TV hung from the ceiling in front of Mina's bed. Zary turned it on. There was no news about the incident on the first two channels. The third channel showed the shooting. The injured guard had died at the scene and they had arrested the shooter on the spot. They showed his picture time after time: a young man with a face so soft you could not think hair had ever grown on it.

There was no more commotion outside, but the police still guarded the clinic.

ABC's local news at one showed a short report, which included images of Mina and Zary entering the clinic. What would happen if they showed the same footage in the afternoon? Everybody would see them! Hamid and Shirin, Khanum Bahadori and Farideh. She had not told anyone about the abortion. Was it a boy? Or a girl? She had killed her own baby! Tear came to her eyes.

She rubbed her belly. It was flat and empty. How would she respond to Hamid? She had killed the baby he had so badly wanted. She had killed Hamid's son and Shirin's brother! She rubbed her belly again. Zary noticed.

"Don't worry my dear, fortunately the fetus was still too small; it hadn't formed into a baby yet," Zary said with a kind comforting voice.

Tears streamed down Mina's face. Zary wiped the tears with the tip of her finger and kissed Mina's face, "you still have time. You can be pregnant again when you are ready for it."

Except for some gray streaks in the front, Zary's hair was still as dark as before, the color that Mina's hair had been. Mina stroked her own hair, very light brown with the streaks of blond highlights. A fake blond! Zary must have noticed the changes.

It took Mina one more hour to grow steady enough to leave the clinic. Zary threw her jacket over Mina's head and helped her exit from the back door.

• • •

Zary's boyfriend, Bernard, was leaving for a long trip to Mexico and Zary had thrown a goodbye party for him. She invited Mina to the party. "You can bring your husband if you want." Mina wasn't that excited to introduce them to each other.

A few days after the clinic incident, Mina had mentioned to Hamid she had found her friend Zary from Iran. Hamid did not show any interest in meeting her. Hamid was not into politics or other social activities; he only cared for his family and his work.

Mina called Zary to say she could not go, but Zary insisted, "Please come, I need your help. Bring a Persian meal with you. Did I tell you that the dinner is potluck? We are going to have a real international dinner; Persian, American, Cuban, Nicaraguan, Palestinian, Lebanese and Egyptian. Try to bring something cold. I don't have enough space to warm up food."

If Mina knew, she would have gone shopping earlier. She looked in the fridge and in the pantry. She had enough ingredients to cook *kuku sabzi*. She unfroze a pack of chopped Persian chives in the microwave, something Khanum Bahadori had forbidden. In a large bowl, she broke six large eggs and beat them with a fork, then added the chive, a small amount of ground meat, some crushed walnut and a handful of *zereshk* that Mother had sent from Iran. She added enough salt and black pepper and mixed them thoroughly. She had learned this style of *kuku sabzi* from Iran Khanum. She tasted the seasoning, and added some more ground black pepper. Then she heated two spoonful of vegetable oil in a non-stick skillet, and when hot enough, she poured in the mixture and cooked it over a low heat until it was set. Afterwards, she cut the *kuku* into wedges, turned over the pieces, and cooked their other side for another fifteen minutes. Now both sides were golden brown.

"I am going to Zary's house to meet a mutual friend of ours who has come from Europe. Don't wait for me. Your dinner is in the oven." She posted the note for Hamid on the fridge.

Mina placed the *kuku* in a round dish, grated some feta cheese over it, and left home.

• • •

It took more than one hour to drive to Zary 's apartment downtown, just couple of blocks from Hotel Bonaventure.

Under the murky street lamps, Mina could see garbage scattered across the sidewalks along the edges of the street. Finding a place to park was more difficult than finding the building. She did not dare to park on the street; on every corner stood a few odd looking people. Three homeless men slept against the wall covering themselves in soiled blankets. On another corner, a young couple accompanied by a small dog, lay together on a ragged feather comforter. Two stray dogs stood over a collapsed trash bag digging food.

Zary had said there was a bank parking lot one block past the building where she could park. A bare footed, ragged man stopped her in front of the lot. His light-colored tangled hair reached his shoulders and a thin beard and long mustache covered his toothless mouth.

"May I help you?" A smell of mixed alcohol, cigarette, and decayed teeth assaulted Mina.

Mina looked at him in surprise. "I want to park here," she said hesitantly.

"Five dollars if you park, ten if I do it for you," the man said seriously. Mina got the point.

"How about if I pay you fifty cents, and park the car myself? "

"One buck!" The man stretched his hand, palm up. His nails were long and dirty.

"Ok, done!"

Mina gave him four quarters. He pocketed the money happily, said "God bless you!" and disappeared into the darkness. Mina mumbled, "God bless America."

• • •

The elevator was not working. She had to climb the spiral staircase; the entire six floors. The door to one of the two flats, facing each other, was open and three men and a woman stood there smoking. They told her she was in the right place. Mina left the dish on the table and went to Zary. Zary introduced her to her friends.

"This is Alice," Alice looked friendly and sweet. "Hey Michael come and meet Mina, my friend from Iran." "Here is Guillermo. Guillermo is Bernard's old friend. He just came back from Nicaragua."

With a square face, short neck, and dark copper complexion, Guillermo looked like an Aztec warrior. His accent reminded Mina of Carlos. He was telling Alice and Michael about his return to Nicaragua years ago, right after Sandinistas came to power. He was now back in the US, looking for financial support for Sandinistas in the upcoming election.

Zary went to meet two new guests and came back with them in a short while.

"Yousef Abdolah, an old friend of Bernard. And Mohammad ..."

She turned to the second man and continued, "Sorry I did not get your last name."

Before Mohammed could answer, Yousef Abdolah said, "My friend Mohammed Ata. He just arrived in the US."

Guillermo turned to Mohamad Ata and said, "Welcome to America, land of opportunity! Where are you coming from?"

Mohammad shook hand with Guillermo and Michael, then turned to Guillermo and said: "I am from Egypt, but I am living and studying in Germany." He ignored Mina who had stretched her hand to him.

Alice and Mina exchanged glances. Alice looked surprised. Mina smiled timidly, pulled up her eyebrow, and shrugged.

"Are you here for a short visit?" Michael asked.

"Maybe. I don't know yet. I will go to Miami next week to..."

Mina did not hear the rest of the conversation. Zary had called her. "Mina would you come here to meet Bernard?" Bernard was a red-haired Canadian lawyer with a pale freckled complexion, and bright green eyes. In three days he was leaving for Mexico City to round up his PhD on anthropology while working on his Spanish. "Please help yourself with drinks," said Bernard after welcoming her.

Zary and Mina were the only Iranians at the party. Mina poured some red wine into a clear plastic cup for herself. Hamid hated plastic cups; he was fanatic about drinking wine in long-stemmed goblets. After getting some food, she returned to Zary and Bernard. There were a couple of new people standing with them. Mina didn't feel like socializing with more new people. She glanced at the previous group. They were engaged in a hot conversation. She waited until she saw Mohammad Ata and Michael leave the group. She then went and stood by Alice. Alice, Guillermo, and Youssef were still entangled in their hot headed discussion about politics. Mina stayed quiet and listened. For years, she had not been involved in the politics of the day, and could no longer take part in these kinds of conversations. Many events had happened in the world while she was busy cooking *fesenjoon* and roulette.

"Mina come here please," Zary called her from across the dinner table.

"Michael wants to know what's in this dish. Please tell him how you made it."

Michael was tall with the bluest eyes ever and brown hair. He stared at Mina with a compassionate curious look. Mina blushed. She couldn't believe someone in this crowd would be interested in her *kuku sabzi*.

Zary left them alone and went to greet a new group; three young Latin American men and a young woman, each carrying a musical instrument.

• • •

Mina stopped dancing and asked, "What time is it?" Michael smiled playfully, "Time for Cinderella to go home!"

"No! It can't be 12! How fast it passed, but you are right; I have to go home."

Although the party was still in full swing, Mina had to leave. She felt a bit off balance and dizzy. She was not used to drinking that much wine, and it was the first time she had danced in presence of so many strangers. Now she had learned some Palestinian dance moves, some Latin American Salsa, and had taught, with Zary's assistance, some Kurdish dance steps to the others, although it was only her second time dancing Kurdish. Hamid had tried to teach her the dance, however Mina danced so clumsily that Hamid and Shirin laughed and teased her for a long time.

Michael walked her to her car. "It was nice to meet you tonight. I had a good time."

"Me too. It was fun."

"Can I have your number?"

Mina hesitated.

"Can we meet again?" Michael probably saw the

question in her eyes.

Mina couldn't think of a word to say. Michael guessed: "Can we do that? Can we go out for dinner sometime?"

Mina panicked, "Oh, no. I am married!" Michael smiled. He seemed disappointed.

Before Mina left the parking lot Michael approached her. She rolled down the window. Michael bent closer and asked, "Do all Iranian women take off their wedding rings when they go to a party without their husbands?" He paused for a moment, and then continued, "Or wearing a ring is one of those western customs that you don't believe in?" he sounded disappointed.

Mina touched her left hand. Michael was right. She had taken off her ring and put it in her purse right before the dance started. She wasn't sure why she had done it. She drove home as fast as she could. It was five past one when she turned to the street where she could see the bedroom window. The light was still on. She parked in the garage and went in.

The first floor was quiet and dark. After slipping off her shoes, she tiptoed to the kitchen and turned on the light above the stove. With her purse still dangling from her shoulder she went to the coffee maker, filled the filter with ground coffee and set it to turn on at 6 am Then, without going to Shirin's room, as she usually did, she went upstairs.

Midway up, she thought of something and returned to the kitchen. She looked for Hamid's favorite cup among the coffee mugs, put it next to the coffee maker, and went back upstairs.

The bedroom light was off now. Hamid seemed

asleep, his back to the door. *He must be awake*, she thought. *He could not have gone to sleep so fast*. Mina snuck to the bathroom, changed her clothes, and went to the bed without bothering to wash off her makeup. Hamid did not stir.

• • •

The smell of stale coffee filled the bedroom. Mina glanced at the clock. Twenty five after nine. She jumped up, pulled on her robe, and went downstairs. The coffee mug was untouched and the coffee pot filled with a dull dark brown coffee. The breakfast table was clean. Hamid usually prepared breakfast for Shirin and himself, and Mina cleaned the table after they left. They hadn't had breakfast. She turned off the coffee maker and went back upstairs, took a quick shower, put on her suit, and pushed her makeup bag into her purse. She could not find the car key on the dresser where she always left it. It wasn't inside her purse either. She must have left it in the car.

The door to the garage was locked. She turned the knob up and down a few times. It didn't open. How could it be? Who had locked it? It *must be* an accident!

She turned back and went to the entry door. It was locked too! How could this happen? Both doors were locked! It couldn't be an accident. Hamid? No. No. Hamid could not do that. It was impossible!

She returned to the living room. Left her briefcase and purse on the floor and sat over the white sheet covering the sofa. She still couldn't figure out what had happened. Hamid's mother flashed in her mind! Oh no!

Oh no!

Panicked, Mina hurried to the phone and picked it up. She changed her mind in middle of dialing 911. What would she say to them? Her father-in-law had killed her mother-in-law twenty five years ago, and now she was worried her husband would do the same? How stupid.

She picked up the phone again and dialed Hamid's work number. Hamid's partner answered.

"Hello Mr. Homayoon. How are you? This is Mina." She did not wait for him to answer. "Is Hamid there?"

"Hello, Miss Mina. He was here this morning but left half an hour ago. Is there anything I can help you with?" He sounded concerned.

Mina heard the key turning in the front door.

"Oh no, thanks. I have to go, I will talk to you later, bye."

Hamid opened the door and entered. Mina stayed motionless. He looked at Mina, standing in the living room, then lowered his head and went to the kitchen to the coffee maker. He poured himself some cold coffee and warmed it in the microwave, then came toward Mina and sat in front of her.

They both stayed still for a while.

"Where were you last night?" he said in English.

Mina lifted her head and looked at him in surprise. He always talked to Mina in Farsi.

"I was at Zary's," she said.

"Until one o'clock in the morning?" he said sarcastically.

"I left at twelve. It took me one hour to get home." Mina tried to stay calm.

"What were you doing in someone's home until 12?"

Hamid was quite upset now. "Someone whom I don't know. Who else was there?"

"I know her," she lost her patience and shouted loudly. "There is no need for you to approve my friends!" Mina's fear was gone.

Hamid jumped up and shouted, "Is she the one who encouraged you to kill your baby? The one who took you to that slaughter house to kill *my son*?"

Mina jolted up. How did Hamid know Zary was with her in the clinic? He had not seen Zary yet! Had he? Shirin! She must have told him. Shirin must have seen the reports shown on TV and recognized Zary among them.

Mina was now extremely angry. She sprang from the sofa and roared in English, "I can't believe it, I can't believe..." Then she continued in Farsi: "Now you make her spy on her mother? What a great father!"

Hamid lost his control and leapt at her: "You... You..." He could not utter the word he wanted to say and shouted in Farsi: "Aren't you ashamed of yourself? The smell of alcohol and cigarettes filled the bedroom when you got into bed." Still holding the coffee mug, his hand rose while he was coming closer to Mina. Mina stepped back, covering her head with her hands.

Hamid's hand stopped halfway. He threw the mug at the sliding door. The glass shattered with a shockingly loud noise.

Startled, they both stared at the tiny pieces of glass blanketing the living room and the patio. A brown line of coffee ran from where Mina stood to the broken glass door.

Hamid turned away and left.

Mina's Revolution

TIJUANA

<u>Jan. 1995</u>

Zary and Mina sat on two chairs at the small table on the sidewalk, facing the ocean. Although tired, they both felt content. After twenty years, they still had the same energy to walk for hours. With Zary, Mina could forget about her daily quarrels with Hamid. With Zary she could go back to the world far away; a world with all its sweet and bitter memories; all of its up and downs. Still that world seemed more real to her than her current life, a world she had a role in, even if a small one.

Mina ordered a nonfat café latté and Zary an organic coffee with a glass of soymilk. Zary was quite excited about her upcoming trip to Mexico City to visit Bernard after six months. She had planned to go there with some of their mutual friends.

"Why don't you come with us?" Zary surprised

Mina with her question. "Some of us will go to Cuba after visiting Mexico. It is easy to go to Cuba from there."

"Me? oh... no, I can't do that..." Mina felt uncomfortable.

"Why not?" Zary asked.

"I have so much to do... what would I do with Hamid and Shirin? ... No, I don't have time, it is impossible..." She tried to think of another reason, but stayed soundless.

"Don't make excuses. Get a week off from work, add two weekends to that, and you will have nine days, a nice exciting vacation. Leave Shirin with her father," Zary said as if it was the easiest thing in the world to do.

Mina had not told Zary about the problems she was having at home. Hamid had not yet forgiven her for *slaughtering* his son. Shirin, too, was mad at her. Her brother was *slaughtered*! Everybody has a brother or sister, *bejoze man.*" She would say, *'bejoze man'* instead of "except me' to make Mina feel guiltier. As if talking in Farsi would affect Mina more. "If I had a brother or sister, your head would get hot with him and not bother me so much." The way she used the phrase "your head would get hot" was a wrong use of the Farsi idiom, which meant she would be too busy to pester Shirin. Mina usually laughed at her language mistakes and changed the subject: "My head never gets 'hot,' it gets warm!" Shirin, frustrated, shouted at Mina, "I wish daddy would divorce you, and make *us* free of you." Her pronunciation of the word "divorce" in Farsi was totally wrong, but Mina did not laugh; the word "*us*" brought her to tears.

Regardless of Hamid's complaints, Khanum Bahadori sounded kind and ready to help. "My poor daughter, how could you do that to yourself? How could you let those strangers to slaughter your baby?" "My daughter, having another baby at home is good for you and Shirin. You have to keep a man at home by busying him with something; otherwise, he will busy himself with stuff outside of the house. Shirin will grow up soon and leave, then you will feel lonely if you don't have another child." She sounded calm. When one day Mina left the room without saying a word to her, Khanum Bahadori finally stopped her words of wisdom.

Mina had never thought of a vacation without Shirin and Hamid. Actually, it wasn't a bad idea. She had always wanted to go to Cuba. When Hamid took them on a Caribbean cruise, their ship circled Cuba and stopped at the nearby islands. She had told Hamid about her wish to go there but he reacted as if Mina said something stupid. How many times had she and the other students in college discussed the Cuban revolution? Castro and Che Guevara were their idols, and going to Cuba was everybody's dream. She had loved the posters of Che and Castro at Parviz's apartment. Thoughts of Parviz made her more nostalgic. She remembered when he came to her apartment, devastated, asking for help. She still felt guilty. She could have offered him to stay for a while. After his visit, she had always kept some money on hand in case he showed up again. He never did. She had asked Zary if she knew more about Parviz's final days and his death. Zary didn't. She was captured and imprisoned right after Parviz's disappearance.

Although they were good comrades in Iran, Zary and Mina never knew each other well, so she might not tell Mina things even if she knew. Mina, too, never talked to Zary about her personal life. She didn't tell her about her affair with Mohsen, and the only thing she said about Hamid was that he was a good person and provided a comfortable home and shelter for his family.

What was wrong with her? She had not had a close friend since Maryam Aliabadi left school at fifteen, to marry her cousin. If they met again, they most likely would not even recognize each other. Zary was the only friend she had left; the only remnant from her past, from her youth. Zary's friends even were becoming her first none Iranian friends. In the past six months, Mina had seen Guillermo and Michael one more time at Zary's, and Liz and Michael another time at Alice's.

"There is a note in my passport that says going to Cuba is illegal. How do you get a visa?" Mina was surprised by her own questions.

"Don't worry about that. They don't stamp your passport in Mexico City or in Cuba. Just don't talk about it with anyone." Zary sounded like an expert.

No, there was no way she could go. She was not planning to go. She had enough troubles with Shirin and Hamid the way things were now. But this could take her away from them for a few days to think. Going to the country that had been so much part of her youth could help her to figure herself out a bit. This could be the vacation she craved for and needed. Thinking of a vacation brought a bittersweet smile to her face.

"Hey Zary, have I told you about my first trip to the North with my family?"

"No, you never tell me anything! I don't know anything about your family."

Mina was surprised Zary was interested to know about her family. She told Zary all about the episode at Motel Qoo. She even told her about Father's obscene words, the frightened face of Ali agha and Mother's humiliation. With each detail, they chuckled hard. Zary was almost in tears. Mina was so charged up she told her about the whole vacation. About Hotel Sedaghat_e No, her amazement at Tehran, and about how all seven of them squeezed into that small car and drove through Iran, from south to north. Mina now couldn't remember the model of the car. She could also hardly remember what the story of The Razor's Edge was, though now she knew how to pronounce the author's name. The only image from the book that remained in her mind was of the protagonist coming back from a long trip, and his old lover, now married to his close friend, staring at his strong hands while the three of them drove somewhere.

Before they parted, Mina asked one more question. Who else was going?

Not that many, the usual gang, you know most of them. Liz, Michael, ...

● ● ●

They arrived in Mexico City shortly past one pm. They had all flown from LAX; Mina, Zary, Michael, Liz, and Guillermo. Bernard waited for them at the airport.

After having lunch at a local restaurant, he took them to his apartment, a large flat located in a poor, working-class neighborhood. They all had dinner at

223

Plaza de la República, then visited *Monumento a la Revolución*, and went back to the airport to pick up Martina, Guillermo's wife. She had flown there from Managua.

The next day Bernard took Mina's passport along with Michael's and Liz's to the Cuban consulate, and got them their visas. Seeing the stapled paper, with a visa stamp, in her passport, made Mina relax. Now she was sure she could tear the visa out of her passport , and get back into the United States with no hassle.

The three days Mina spent in Mexico City were among the best of her life. She had never appreciated so many paintings, concerts, and dances. The city was full of murals, which made the whole city look like an art museum. The artwork Mina liked the most was Diego Rivera's famous mural at the Palace of Fine Arts, a strange work called *Man, Controller of the Universe.* The center of the mural looked like a movie poster for The *Time Machine* and showed a man in control of the universe with confidence and power. In the corners were pictures of Vladimir Lenin.

Mina liked to see Frida Kahlo's original painting, copies of which she had seen at Zary's and Alice's homes. Instead, Michael took them to see Trotsky's grave and monument at the back of Frida's museum.

• • •

In the immigration office line at the Cuban Jose Marti International Airport, Mina stood next to Liz and Michael. The line was short, 14 or 15 people, mostly Mexican. They were supposed to meet the tour guide in the lobby, who would take them to their hotel to meet with the rest of the group; Zary, Bernard, Guillermo, and Martina.

"There might be some more people you know," Zary told Mina and added bitingly: "I don't want you to mention to anyone that you saw them on this trip."

Mina had overheard Mohammad Ata and Youssef Abdullah's names. She did not like either of them. Whenever they showed up at any of the parties, she avoided them as much as she could. She had had enough of fanatics.

"Next," called the Immigration officer looking at Liz in front of Michael.

Michael held the tail of Liz's loose blouse and faced Mina. "Ladies first!"

Mina looked at their faces, both smiling. Liz was tall with a body almost twice as big as Mina's. Zary had told her that Liz had recently separated from her longtime girlfriend.

"Liz, never mind him, please keep going!" said Mina.

Liz smacked Michael's hand, freed her blouse and went to the immigration kiosk. It didn't take more than couple of minutes for the officer to let her pass. He called for the next person in line.

"After you ma'am!" said Michael, posing theatrically, facing Mina and extending his arm toward the kiosk.

Mina took a close look at Michael. In his blue jeans and gray shirt, the blue of his eyes looked grayish. More handsome than ever.

"Mike, what is going on today? You have become a sexist clown at the entrance of a communist country." and pushed him ahead.

"Hey, hey, watch it lady! You're a Muslim woman," said Michael with a sweet frown. "You should never touch a man who is not your husband!"

He looked even sweeter now.

"Hey you guys, stop flirting! Come on Mike, he is waiting for you!" Liz called from the other side of the immigration booth.

Michael proceeded to the booth but before he handed his passport to the officer, Liz cried, "Oh my God! He stamped my passport!" She was examining her passport.

Michael withdrew his passport. "Are you sure?" he asked Liz. "He is not supposed to mark our passports."

"But he did! It is here in my passport. We are fucked!" Liz said angrily. Michael turned to the officer and talked to him in a broken Spanish. Then moved back from him and said, "He says he has to stamp our passports, otherwise we can't enter the country."

Mina was terrified. How could she go back to America? She was not ready for this one. She had not told Hamid and Shirin she was going to Cuba. She was supposed to be in Florida for a business-training course. They didn't know she was with Zary and her friends.

"Did you tell him we'll get in trouble if he stamps our passports?"

"Yes, he knew it. I don't think he gives a damn about Americans anyway."

"Should we talk to his supervisor?"

"I asked him that too. He said it is the law."

"What should we do?"

"Let's go in. We can return to the US from Tijuana," Michael responded. "They won't check our passports there."

Oh no, I can't take this risk, America is the only country I've got! Where can I go if they throw me out of there? "You can go ahead and join the others. I'll return to Mexico."

"C'mon. Don't be a chicken! Let's go in. I promise to take you back to the U.S. unharmed."

"*No*, I don't want to do that," Mina was damn serious. "I am going back to the States."

"So, let me stay with you and make sure the airline will take you back to Mexico City."

"That's alright; I can take care of myself. You go ahead. The tour guide is waiting for you."

"I am so sorry. Are you sure you are going to be OK?"

"Oh, yes, yes don't worry about me. I am a big girl now! I can find my way back."

He gave her a friendly hug. "OK, good luck! I am going now."

Before he got to the immigration office Mina called him, "Mike!"

Michael turned back and watched her with the clearest eye Mina had ever seen. Mina's face flushed.

"Write down my phone number. Call me if you need a lift from Tijuana."

"Thanks, that would be great!"

He paused for a second, then excitedly said, "Why don't you wait in Mexico City until we come back? It's only three days!"

Three more days in Mexico City!

"Find a hotel and have fun. You know when we are coming back. Come to the airport, we will change our tickets and go back to the States together through

Tijuana," he said enthusiastically.

Not a bad idea. She always wanted to have couple of days to herself to do things she wanted to do.

The first day back in Mexico City Mina went to see Casa Azul, Frida Kahlo's house and museum. The original paintings were amazing; all vivid and alive; self-portraits dominating her rages and sufferings. Just like Forough Farrakhzad, Mina's favorite poet, who did the same in her poems. They both cried out their inner world and pains in their works, works of art that touched the life of many in the world. Two artists from two sides of the world who created their masterpieces at almost the same age as Mina was, when she was cooking and cleaning, trying to make an impression on Khanum Bahadori, and playing the role of a good housewife. She wasn't even successful at it; her *fesenjoon* never came out as good as Khanum Bahadori's!

• • •

Three days later Mina and Michael were in Tijuana. They both had left their suitcases with Zary to ship them to LA. Zary stayed with Bernard in Mexico City.

They took an old rattletrap taxi to Avenida Revolución, the heart of Tijuana's tourist district. Mike knew every corner of TJ.

They planned to stroll across the border after visiting the city and having dinner. On the other side of the border they could take a taxi to the train station, and go to LA. Walking through immigration office did not require a passport. They could show their driver's license or other IDs to cross the border.

Packed with throngs of people, Avenida Revolución evoked in Mina's mind a distant memory of Lalezaar and Topkhanaeh Square.

Little boys and girls rushed to sell them knick-knacks; chewing gum, flowers, cheap handcrafts and silver plated jewelries. Stores sold leather goods, blankets, and other souvenirs of Mexico. Short Indian women with straight dark hair framing their round faces – seemingly sitting neckless on their shoulders – carried babies on their backs while being surrounded by more children of every size and age. Some of them spread their art crafts out before them to sell to passersby. Car horns diverted Mina's attention every few seconds. As they approached the center of the street, they saw more signs of bars and liquor stores on both sides. Loud booming music came from the speakers and filled the street. In the entrances of the bars, men with welcoming smiles invited them to go in. The bars were full of young men and women, and even some teenagers, who came from America to spend the weekend in town. Photographs of half-naked women appeared in some windows.

A small boy of seven or eight carrying necklaces and earrings approached Mina and pulled on her blouse. Mina stopped. The boy immediately separated a necklace from the bunch hanging from his hand and offered it to her. "For you *Señora*, good for you."

Mina smiled, patted the boy's head, and continued on her way. Michael stopped and asked the price.

"For you ten dolores," said the boy innocently.

Michael fetched a ten-dollar bill and paid for the necklace.

"A couple of blocks earlier a woman offered me the

same necklace for five dollars," said Mina laughing.

"I am sure if you bargain with them you can even buy it for two dolares! I am sure my government has robbed this little boy and his ancestors much more than that! Now come on, let me hang it on your beautiful neck."

Mina gathered her hair above her neck and Michael fastened the necklace around it. He then put his arms around her shoulder and they walked together. Mina enjoyed the warmth of his body.

Some blocks further, at the intersection of the Revolución and Constitución, two men stood next to a stair leading down to a bar. Each man had a bottle of Tequila in his hand and a small whistle in his mouth. They wore white aprons and carried white towels. One of them blew his whistle while raising the bottle of tequila, and pulled Mike toward the stairs. Mina didn't know what was happening. Holding Mina's hand, Michael followed the man down the stairs to a door. As the waiter opened the door, a mixture of humdrum noise, smoke, and the blast of music rushed out. Mina and Michael followed the man to a table on the other side of the bar. It took Mina a while to get used to the dark. The place consisted of a narrow lounge with a bar on the right side and a few tables and chairs on the left. Further back, a band of local musicians played entertaining music around a dance floor.

Another waiter, also blowing in his whistle, joined the first one. The noise was ear piercing. The first waiter raised his hand with tequila and pointed at Mina, grinning. Mina wanted to know what was going on. Michael nodded to the man and laughed. "Nothing, just having fun. Don't panic !Just relax and enjoy it." The waiter went behind Mina, looped his arm around her neck loosely, pulled her head back, and poured a few drops of tequila into her mouth. Next, he drizzled in some lime and sprinkled salt, put the towel on her mouth, and shook her head. Michael and the people around laughed hard.

"Gulp it down; he just made a margarita for you!" Michael shouted joyfully.

Mina, now understanding what was going on, swallowed the drink. The waiter stepped behind Michael and with the shake of his hand sought Mina's permission. Mina, with a lively laugh, gave him her approval. The waiter made another Margarita!

Music played deafeningly. Michael pointed to the waiters and showed Mina to them.

"No, no, no..." Mina shook her head, and pushed the men back. Michael walked to her and held her hands while the waiters did their job.

After a couple of rounds of making margaritas, the waiters got their tips and left the two of them to themselves.

The band was playing slow music. Michael took Mina's hand and guided her to the dance floor. He put his arm around her waist, laid his face on her face, and they danced to the end of music.

It was fantastic. She had never experienced such happiness and excitement in her life.

In the next two hours, the waiters came back a few more times and played the game of margarita making in their mouths. Mina was tipsy, and totally into the game. Even when the men were busy at other tables, she called and asked them to make margaritas, and screamed, along with other people, "More, more, more..."

On their way up the stairs, Mike put his arms around her neck, pulled her face to his and kissed her repeatedly. Mina kissed him back.

A few blocks away, in front of a restaurant, a group of mariachis played a joyful music. Young couples occupied all the tables and chairs. Mina and Michael listened to the music holding hands. The mariachis dressed in silver studded costumes, short jackets, high tight black pants, and wide brimmed hats, played violins, guitars, basses, and trumpets. Just like the movies when they stood outside the woman's window and sang love songs. The rhythms and the orchestration of the music made it very enjoyable. She had read somewhere that mariachis' songs spoke about love, betrayal, death, politics and revolutionary heroes. She could feel all of those in their music.

The musicians neared them while playing the music. The singer was an old man, his face full of hollow dips, his small eyes veiled under bushy black eyebrows, his hair greying at the temples. Two gold teeth showed in his face when he smiled. Michael said something in Spanish to him when he finished his singing. He exchanged words with the rest of the group, and when they came to an agreement, they started to sing. Mina moved closer to Michael and their warm bodies touched. Michael translated part of the song for her. It was *Bella María de Mi Alma*, Beautiful Maria of My Soul, considered the most romantic song in Spanish.

A neon sign blinked above the door next to the restaurant, "Hotel *Magnífico.* "

"It is getting late, how about if we stay here tonight

and leave for LA tomorrow morning?" Michael asked. His question carried many unasked questions. An image of Carlos asking her to go to his friend's party flashed in front of Mina's eyes. She nodded.

They entered the hotel through a narrow hallway. Michael exchanged some words with the receptionist. The man looked into a notebook laid on the desk, "... *un quarto con* two beds, *y uno con one* Queen bed?"

Michael glanced at Mina. She looked away.

"The Queen Bed, *por favor.*"

Their room was on the second floor above the restaurant.

• • •

Michael got up and walked to the bathroom. He was entirely naked, his body hairless, his muscles strongly built; a small foreskin covered the tip of his penis. Mina, too, was naked. She pulled the sheet over her body, then sat down and looked for her clothes; they all were scattered around the bed on the floor. Michael turned on the bathroom light and went inside. Mina could hear the sound of peeing and then the loud sound of the toilet flushing.

He returned to bed, slipped next to Mina under the sheet, and put his hand on her breast. Mina turned to him and kissed his lips. Michael caressed her cheeks and lips, "You are so beautiful."

Mina smiled. Michael pulled Mina's hair away from her face. "What is this scar on your forehead?"

Mina raised her hand and touched the remains of the old wound. "Nothing important, just a memorable gift from my countrymen."

She then told him about the Woman's Day protest and the stones flying to the air.

"Oh, I get it !You were one of those who turned against Khomeini right after the Revolution!"

Mina looked at him with surprise.

"Oh, no, no that wasn't it. Many women were there. Most of them were not even into politics," said Mina as she remembered the day. "We went there to object to the mandatory hijab."

"But that was so soon! You should have waited! It was...what...just a month or two after the Revolution?" said Michael while gently touching her face. "Just a month after that glorious uprising!? Right after he stood up to American Imperialism and their puppet, the Shah?"

Mina felt she had to defend herself and the other women. "We had to do something. He changed all his promises. We were not expecting to have to cover ourselves head to toe with a chador!"

"Don't forget his effect on the region and how he opened the door for more struggles and oppositions in the Middle East. In Egypt, in Afghanistan, and even in other parts of the world. He gave hope to the struggle in Palestine. It's true that women's rights and struggles are important to them, but what does it matter if the whole society is oppressed? A country needs to be free and independent before it starts to restore women's civil rights."

Mina recalled the first time she met Michael in Zary's house. He had not even noticed that Mohammad Ata refused to shake hand with Mina and Alice; or maybe he saw it but chose to ignore it.

Michael moved away Mina's hair from her face again, and then kissed the lesion above her eyebrow, "Let's sleep now. We can continue our conversation tomorrow on the way home. There is so much you need to learn about politics." He then turned his back to her, and soon began to breathe steadily.

Mina turned toward the window. The fluorescent light of the hotel's sign, *Magnifico*, winked from outside. She could not sleep. She got up, wrapped her body in the sheet, and went to the window. She looked down at the street. It was still busy, but there were no Mariachis. She looked at the clock inside the room. One hour past midnight. Michael lay on his stomach, breathing calmly.

Mina picked up the pieces of her clothing and tiptoed to the bathroom. She put them on, picked up her purse, and left the room.

The restaurant was still open.

"Buenas noches, Señora. Es usted que cena?" said the barman, a broad smile on his face.

"I am not Mexican, I *do not* speak Spanish," Mina responded, irritated.

She pulled a chair out from behind a table and sat. She then ordered a hot tea. She now felt guilty for acting angrily toward the waiter. She wasn't pissed off by him, but felt generally angry and impatient. Why had Michael defended the Islamic government? What did *he* know about that ruthless regime? Hadn't Zary told him about her ordeals inside and outside of the prison? Anti-imperialism! Was that enough? What about the women who had to live under that barbaric *anti-imperialist* regime? The day she and other women went to the streets to protest the mandatory hijab, her male colleagues, too, told them defending women's rights was not a priority. Was it important to them at all? When she told Mohsen about her pregnancy he wanted her to dispose of the baby: *We have more important things to worry about!* What was the difference between Mohsen and Michael? Oh yes, there was one difference! Mohsen and his comrades very soon became victims of that government, but there was no real danger threatening Michael and his Trotskyist friends. Let the Islamic rulers do whatever they wanted to the women! Yes, an anti-imperialist regime was a good subject of discussion among the so-called intelligentsia at their parties while they stood around drinking wine and having a good time.

It felt strange to compare Michael with Mohsen. Except for their shared political beliefs, what was their resemblance? Although they both played an important role in her life – somehow similar – they were very different. Mohsen was the first man who had made love with her. *love?* He had never tried to please her. Michael was the first one showing her the joy of sexual pleasure, the joy of having an orgasm. Even thinking of those moments of excitement made her feel joyful and long for Michael. Why had she deprived herself of such enjoyment for so long? If she had just gone to that party with Carlos ten years ago, or if she had not accepted Hamid's proposal, she could have experienced it long ago. Now, after so many years when she was over forty, she had just discovered that pleasure. All those years of her youth, all those years that she could have had that happiness, that free, unlimited gift of nature, she even didn't know what she was missing. If Hamid had not been so shy in bed, or if he didn't get so nervous when they made love, could their relationship be different? Maybe she was the one to blame. She had never looked at their togetherness as a love affair. Except for her childhood infatuation with him, she never had any affection for him the way she did for Carlos and Michael. Her heart never beat when she was with him. He was so different from her. The love for Shirin was the only thing they had in common. Why hadn't she tried to make it work? Was it because she never wanted to enjoy him, to enjoy making love with him? Why? Whom was she punishing? Hamid? Herself? Or maybe Shirin, who had so badly wanted her to marry him? But Shirin was only a child, a child yearning for a father and a happy family. Who was really to blame? Wasn't she herself as guilty of this crime against herself? Maybe the real crime was being so pathetically frail, so pitifully lame. How did she become so weak? She stood for herself when she was much younger; she resisted Bahram's marriage proposal. Was it because she became a mother? A mother who sacrificed her life for her child's?

For the first time in fourteen years, she clearly, and without resentment, was thinking about her affair with Mohsen and her marriage to Hamid. Bad feelings could disappear if she did not engage with them. It was simple. Just deny them and they vanish. Maybe Mohsen had never existed. Perhaps he was only a bad dream, a nightmare, punishment for not listening to Mother, not listening or considering the beliefs and customs of her society, her ancestors.

The clock showed it was a quarter to two. Except for

her and the barman-waiter, no one was in the restaurant. As he saw her looking around, he brought her the bill for the one hot tea she had ordered. Mina left a dollars for him and went back to the hotel.

She didn't have a key! She knocked at the door gently, and waited. No response from inside. She knocked again and waited for couple more minutes. There was silence everywhere. She turned away to go to the office to get a key, but stopped half way in stairs. *What did she need the key for*? She sat on one of the steps thinking. Within few minutes she made her mind. She opened her handbag and searched for a piece of paper. The only loose paper she could find was the white form with the stamp of the Cuban entry visa attached to her passport. She took it out and wrote on the back of it.

Dear Michael,
I left for Los Angeles. Sorry for leaving like this.

She read the line, then ripped off the paper from under the line, threw the top part away and wrote:

My dear Michael,
Thanks very much for everything. I really had a good time with you here, but I have to leave. I cannot handle one more fanatic, even one as cute and well-mannered as you.

She signed and folded the form. Before she pushed the letter under the door, she opened the fold and read her note one more time. She added another line at the end.
Please don't worry about me; I just need to spend

some time alone. I will call you when I get my thoughts together.

She turned away and left.

● ● ●

The taxi driver showed Mina the building of the immigration office, a couple of blocks from the border, and dropped her off at the curbside. Mina paid him and walked in the direction of the border.

Cars crawled in three lines ending at the border. Mina passed street vendors who stopped her now and then, and entered the two-story building. A short line, consisting of a few American men and some Mexican couples, formed in the lobby. An officer checked their legal documents and let them pass the border. Mina looked into her handbag to fetch her passport but could not find it. She opened the half-closed zipper, and looked inside. She sighed loudly. Her passport and wallet were gone! All her documents and money were gone! Someone must have stolen it while she was walking to the building. She was sure she had put the wallet back into her bag after she paid the Taxi.

She spent ten minutes arguing with the guard that she was not Mexican, rather an American citizen with all legal documents who had lost her wallet. *It was not up to him to decide who was legal and who was not.* He sent her to the second floor to the Immigration Office.

● ● ●

Mina stood in line with people waiting to get to the

Immigration Office. Although the line was not long, considering the rate it was advancing, she did not have any hope of getting there in less than half an hour. She was impatient.

An officer with a bushy mustache sat on the other side of a glass window.

"My passport and my wallet with all my identification cards were stolen from me..."

The officer didn't wait for Mina to finish her sentence, "Very original excuse!" he said.

"Sorry officer, but it is true! I got robbed after I got off the Taxi."

"I know, I know...all of you lose your documents!"

"Believe me, I did! Someone took my wallet from my purse. My name is Mina Shabani and I work for a big manufacturing firm in Los Angeles."

"Mina, Maria, whatever, it doesn't matter. Go back, your husband is waiting for you at home!" the officer smirked. He looked above Mina's shoulder and yelled, "Next!"

Mina didn't move. A pudgy girl with a short neck and black straight hair falling to her shoulders, passed Mina and placed herself in front of the glass window. Mina went back to the end of the line. In less than ten minutes, she was in front of the same officer again.

"It's you again!" said the officer with a rude irritated voice. "If you don't leave right away, I'll call the guards to take you back!"

Mina was so angry tears started running down her face. The officer got up from his chair and shouted, "Guard... guard... I need a guard here!" Then looking at the young guard coming toward him from the other side of the saloon, he said, "Please take Maria here back to where she belongs!"

The guard guided Mina to the first floor and toward the exit door on the Mexican side. Tears still kept trickling down her eyes.

It was 4:15 am and people still waited to enter the building. Mina stood at the end of the line again. From where she stood, she could see the big M of the McDonald on the American side of the border. She needed a coffee so badly. She was exhausted and thirsty. There was no way she could wait there another half an hour or get into the building and start another argument with the immigration officers.

She still had couple of Pesos in her purse. She walked away from the building to find a coffee shop. When passing a backstreet, she saw a neon sign for a café and turned into the alley. She had not gone more than a few steps when two men approached her. Two chubby middle-aged men with big bellies and whiskers, stupid grins on their faces.

"Hola Senorita, como estas?" said one of the men, his breath smelling of alcohol and dead fish.

"I am sorry, I don't understand Spanish," she said seriously.

The other man came closer with his smile widening. "You speak English? I speak English. You beautiful. I help you. I have good customer. Pay good dolares!" he said with a heavy accent. Mina looked around. An old plump woman, wearing a short skirt and a tank top, her large breast bulging out, stood against the wall, not paying attention to them. Next to her, a younger man with the stub of a cigarette between his fingers and his eyes closed, squatted on the ground. Another young man stood next to him, watching Mina and the two pimps.

Mina turned and walked out of the alley. She heard the steps of someone fallowing her.

"You American? I have good stuff. Cheap." A man was behind her. He could be the same young man in the alley. Mina ran faster.

She needed to find a bathroom. There was no line in front of the Immigration office. She entered the building and directly went to the women's restroom. After urinating, she stood in front of the mirror and looked at herself. No wonder those pimps were hassling her! Her hair was totally disheveled and her eyes were sleepy and bloated. Mascara smeared under her eyes, and the top button of her blouse was open revealing part of her small breasts. She fastened her button and washed her face. She then combed her hair, held it back with an elastic band she found in her purse, and left the restroom.

She went to the public phone in the lobby, picked up the receiver and looked at the price list above the phone. She needed thirty-seven Pesos to call America. She opened her purse and scanned inside, she found 4 ten Peso coin and deposited them into the box and dialed her home. The phone rang three times.

"Allo...Allo..." Hamid answered. After thirty years being in America, he still forgot where he was when he was awoken up. He answered in Farsi.

His voice was sleepy. Mina looked at the clock. It was 4:35 am. Hamid said a few more Hellos, and hung up.

The same two officers Mina had seen before stood in the lobby and chatted. There was no one else around. After two hours of being inside and outside of the immigration building, she felt she knew everybody and every corner.

She left the building. This time she went directly to the line of the cars waiting behind the border. Unlike hours ago, there were only two short lines. She looked through the windows of the cars and went toward a white Honda Civic at the end of a line.

One couple sat in the front seat and another in the back. Both boys had very short hair, almost shaved, and they looked to be in their late teens.

Mina tapped at the passenger window with her knuckle. The girl in the front row turned toward her and rolled down the window. "Sorry to bother you. Can you give me a lift to the other side of the border?" said Mina, smiling as best as she could.

The girl looked at her and chuckled. The other two people, sitting in the back, started giggling, too.

"Why don't you walk through the border office?"

"I have lost all my documents and they won't let me in. They don't believe me!"

All four of them burst into laughter.

"What makes you think *we* believe you!?" asked the girl in the passenger seat, still laughing.

"Because you are nicer than those assholes!" Mina tried to stay cool.

One of them whistled from the back seat and the rest burst into laughter again. The driver said, "Hey guys, how about smuggling an illegal alien?"

"She's cool, let's do it!" said the girl who sat in the back.

Everybody chuckled.

"Where are you going? To Los Angeles?" the boy

behind the steering wheel asked.

"It would be nice, if you're going there."

"How much should we charge her?" said the boy in the back seat.

"Get in! We're going to the base, in Camp Pendleton," said the driver turning to Mina. "We can drop you off in Oceanside at the train station. It is on our way."

Mina opened the backdoor, hopped in, and sat next to the girl.

Ten minutes later, their car approached the border. The immigration officer waved them to pass, and they drove through the line without inspection.

New York - Shirin

"Ms. Shabani, we are about to land. Would you like to have a glass of milk with a fresh chocolate chips cookie?"

Mina pushed the armchair back to a sitting position and straightened her hair. The sweet smell of the chocolate chips cookies filled the plane: "Oh, yes indeed. They smell marvelous! Do you bake them here?"

"Almost !We have the dough ready; we bake them in the oven. Do you want your milk cold or warm?" asked the flight attendant.

"Warm, please."

Mina picked up the computer, still on the small table next to her, and placed it in its case. John was not in his seat. Mina took out a lipstick and a small mirror, applied a layer of light cherry to her lips, and shaped her hair with the tip of her fingers.

245

John stood couple of rows ahead, his face away from Mina, talking with another passenger. Standing, his body looked more built and tall. He was handsome.

"Ladies and Gentlemen, we will be in New York in a few minutes. Please…" the speaker announced.

As the plane came to a total stop, the flight attendant brought back her jacket and rolling suitcase. Mina said goodbye to John and left the plane.

Right before exiting the airport, she heard John calling her from behind.

"Mina, may I give you a ride to your hotel? My chauffeur is waiting outside the building."

"Thanks John. I am sure a limousine will be waiting for me outside."

Mina looked into the lobby. "Ms. Mina Shabani." A middle-aged fair-haired man wearing a black suit and white shirt held up a placard with her name on it.

"He is here. Thanks for the offer anyhow. Until next time."

Mina went toward the chauffeur. "Good afternoon ma'am. Welcome to New York."

Mina followed him. Then she thought of something and turned back to John.

"If you still want us to meet tomorrow, I can meet you in the evening at the Top of the World in the South Tower."

"Great! I know exactly where it is. What time?"

"I will be there from…" She paused a moment, "Let's meet after the sunset. How about six-thirty?"

"I'll be there gladly. Please call me if anything changes."

"Sure, I will. See you tomorrow."

Mina said goodbye and entered the Limousine.

• • •

The black limousine passed Central Park, turned left onto the Fifth Avenue and stopped in front of the Plaza Hotel. The driver opened the door for Mina, got her suitcase from the trunk and handed it to the doorman who was waiting for them.

"Ms. Shabani?"

"Yes."

"Good evening ma'am. Your room is ready. Please proceed to the courtesy desk to pick up the key to your room."

On the way to the hotel, Mina had called and had checked in.

Her room, with a glass door opening to a balcony, was on the tenth floor. Mina could see the Central Park and the small lake in the middle. She was not ready to go to bed yet. It was just 8 pm in Los Angeles. She picked up the room service menu and ordered a basket of fresh fruits, then removed her laptop from its case and attached the blue Ethernet plug into it. By the time the Internet came up, she lost her interest in checking her emails. She could read them in the morning and glance at the necessary documents for her meeting.

She picked up a cluster of grapes, sat on the bed, turned on the TV, and surfed the channels. The only interesting movie was a comedy she had seen with Zary years ago, before Zary moved out of the States. Where was she now? The first two years after she left, she sent postcards from different countries: Germany,

Yugoslavia, Egypt, Mexico and a few other places. The last card was from Bolivia three years ago, about the same time Mina broke up with Michael for the last time. Anyway, she had been reserved with Mina the last years she was in Los Angeles. She never told Mina where in the world she was moving to, or in her postcards mentioned whether she lived in that country or was only visiting.

Mina finally turned off the TV and lay down in the big king bed with white embroidered sheets. The pillowcases looked like the old-fashioned ones that Mother had made when she was young. She still had some left from her dowry. She showed them to Mina and Mahnaz and promised she would make some for their dowries too. Poor Mother! She had never fulfilled her wish. None of the girls had married the way she wanted. Still, she was so happy when she heard Mina had married Hamid, although she seemed confused about Shirin's age.

It was a long time since Mina had seen Mother. Mahnaz had married a Pakistani man in Sweden. She had published two poetry collections in both Farsi and Swedish, and did not have any children. Father died years ago when Mina was in Mexico with Michael. Mina received the news right when she came back from Tijuana. Although she had never missed him, she mourned his death and regretted not having said a proper goodbye to him. Would it happen with Mother too? Mina had promised her that she would go back home with Shirin one day.

She wanted to show Shirin her homeland, the house in Borazjan where she grew up and where Mother still lived, and the streets of Tehran where she had marched many times. Would she be able to find any of those streets now? Many times she had tried to remember where the Paris cafeteria or Danesh bookstore were located and how she went there from her apartment, or where the American Embassy, one of the last places she visited, was. Now, the city had grown and new highways connected the south to the north and the west to the east. She would get totally lost there. She hardly knew anyone in Tehran anymore. Most of the people she knew were either killed by government, or had escaped, or emigrated. What would have happened to her if she had stayed?

It would even be unsafe for her to travel there now. Although she registered her marriage with the Iranian consulate in Washington, she never registered her divorce with them. Hamid didn't ask for it, and it didn't matter to Mina. She was still married to Hamid under the Iranian law. He could stop her from leaving Iran if he wanted.

He could even get her into serious trouble, maybe even a death penalty or stoning, if he could prove that she had had an affair with someone else. Mina doubted he would do that. Although they were on bad terms, he wasn't that evil. He himself never wanted to go back to Iran. He had left all the bad memories there and didn't want to face them again. He never talked about his mother's murder to anyone. Mina knew how much he suffered from it. She could see the pain in his eyes anytime anyone asked about his childhood. He was terrified when people asked about his parents. After his release from prison, Hamid's father had married again, and had two more children. Hamid never contacted his half siblings.

Hamid was safe with Mina. He guessed Mina and her family had heard the news from his grandmother, but they never talked about it. He tried to re-live a happy childhood with Shirin, who never showed any interest in seeing Iran either. Maybe she was interested now. How would Mina know? She had not seen her in such a long time.

• • •

Right after coming back from Mexico, Mina rented a room from one of her coworkers, a divorcee with two children. Upon Hamid's request, she let Shirin stay with him. On Wednesdays, Mina picked Shirin up from school and spent the evening with her, then took her to Hamid's house before 10 o'clock. Shirin also spent Saturday mornings, and some Sundays with Mina, but she always preferred to go home at nights.

In less than six months, Mina rented a two-bedroom apartment close to Shirin's school. She now made enough money to decorate the apartment the way she wanted. Buying a tall wooden bookcase was the very first thing she did. When she was placing her old books on the shelves, she paused on Forugh Farokhzad's poetry book. She sat down in between the boxes, opened the book and read most of the poems in one sitting.

She then, bought a set of green sofas, and a dark brown wooden dining set. She tossed several cushions here and there – colorful modern cushions that matched the color of her Persian Shirazi klim Mahnaz had sent her. She selected the framed paintings with a lot of care. The one above the sofa was a rectangle watercolor with a pale green background and vivid violet irises spread all over in no particular arrangement. Above the dining table She hung an   abstract image of a woman and two children sitting in front of the ocean, watching the sunset. She soon changed her mind and replaced the painting with a hazy image of the sea. The floor was made of light- colored wood. She spread Mahnaz's klim under the dining table and the Persian rug Mother had sent, in front of the sofa. She had hidden the rug under the bed for several years. Hamid did not like the dark red color of the rug and its Turkmen design. She would not let him or anybody else have control over her life anymore. Finally, she could live the way she wanted. She could take care of Shirin now. She was ready, mentally and financially. She wanted her daughter back.

● ● ●

"Don't even think about it," Hamid was dead serious. "She stays here with me in this very house."

"Do you mean *my* daughter should live with you?" Mina was astonished.

"*Your* daughter? She is *my* daughter as much as she is yours. You don't believe it? Ask her. How much time have you spent with her in the past year? Trust me; it was much less than the time a mother should spend with her child."

You are crazy. You are crazy if you think I will let you have my child. You have no right over her. Shirin is the only one I have in the world. I am not going to let you steal her from me. I am going to take you to court.

The divorce court did not accept her custody request. Shirin was old enough to decide which parent she wanted to live with. "I'll stay with my dad in my home."

"I will disown you if you decide to stay with him," Mina was exceedingly mad. "You don't know anyone called Mina anymore if you do so!"

Later, when she got a hold of herself, she tried to be more logical. "If you live with me, you can see your father anytime you want. You can also spend some weekends with him."

"Mom, I am sorry. I love you so much, but I have to stay with dad."

"How about me? Don't you miss me?"

"I do, I do. It would kill me to think about not seeing you every day, but there's no way I can leave Dad." Her tears streamed down her face while talking. "My dad needs me; I can't live without him either."

Shirin stayed in Hamid's house, or as she called it, "our house." She sobbed hard when she kissed Mina, "Mom, I wish you would come back to your senses and think logically and unselfishly. There is nothing in the world I want, more than for you to come back to our house, and for us all to live together again." She talked to Mina as if she was the mother and Mina was her child!

Logical? What did Shirin knew about logic? If Mina *had thought logically, even for a minute*, she would not have surrendered to Mohsen and his selfish, barbaric lust. If she *had thought logically*, she would have listened to his recommendation and had an abortion. If she *had thought selfishly* she would have never married

Hamid...If... If... Mina erupted into uncontrolled hysterical crying and screaming until she was out of breath.

After all the misery and desolation she had suffered just because of Shirin, now even the American judicial system had questioned her "Motherhood." The Iranian judicial system not only didn't recognize the state of her motherhood, but also refused to give Shirin a birth certificate until someone volunteered to be *her father*! Yeah, really, "Paradise lies under the feet of mothers!" Blah, blah...blah... she should tell Shirin everything. She should tell her about her real father and about Hamid. She would definitely begin to understand Mina better... but, no, she might get deeply hurt. It could be too much for her. Mina could not bring herself to do it. She had already brought a distance between her daughter and herself and she could not take Hamid, the only father she had known, from her as well.

For months, Mina stayed in bed for hours, her thoughts wandering. Would it have been better if she had killed herself that night in the Bonaventure Hotel? What had she gained in the last eight years? She felt lonelier than ever. During those hard times, she at least had Shirin's love. In that meager apartment, with only one bedroom, she hugged Shirin every night and felt her body next to hers. What did she have now? Maybe if she had told Shirin everything, she would've changed her mind. If she knew the high price she had paid for Shirin to have a normal life. If Shirin could remember those years they lived alone, the years she had to work hours in that wretched pitiable restaurant to make a life for them. If she told Shirin about her pregnancy, the period of the ultimate loneliness, the time that her only link to life was Shirin and her graceful movements in her womb, if she told her about all those years that everybody forgot her, the years nobody recognized them officially, not even her own brother and parents. Hamid was the only one who accepted them, both of them, the way they were, and Mina was deeply, from the bottom of her heart, grateful to him. But hadn't she paid her dues to him? How many more years of depriving her of a normal life would be enough for him?

It was all her fault. Why did she never let Shirin know about her feelings toward Hamid? Why did she let the two of them grow so close? Why did she let Hamid steal her daughter, a daughter who was Shirin Sha'abani for years? Didn't Shirin also have a right to know the truth about her past?

No, she would not surrender! She would not give up her daughter, her own daughter! She has to fight back. She has to fight to gain what was hers. She had to do something. Hadn't she done it before? Hadn't she struggled hard with Mother and Father, with her old country's culture and traditions? With her new fellow citizens' biases against immigrants? With Mr. Kumar, with Hossein, even with Mr. and Mrs. Jones? Mina smiled when she remembered the terrified look in their eyes when she emptied the entire coffee pot into their cups. They looked like they had just faced a mad vicious terrorist from the Middle East.

Mina wrote a letter to Shirin. This time she told her everything, everything about Mohsen and Hamid. She even told her the reason she had accepted Hamid's proposal, regardless of her emotions toward Carlos. She told her about all the things she had done for the two of them.

No response from Shirin for two weeks. She sent another letter in case Shirin had not received the first one or Hamid had destroyed it before she saw it. No response again.

Mina hired an expensive lawyer and appealed the court's decision.

"Hamid is the only father I have. I definitely want to live with him," Shirin told the judge. "My father never threatened to leave me if I didn't choose him! My mother did, she said she would never see me again if I stayed with my father! What kind of a mother is she?" She burst into tears many times during the testimony.

"She even killed my child without consulting me. Shirin and I went through a lot of emotional distress because of her selfish actions," Hamid told the judge. "She changed a lot after the abortion, too. She spent long hours out of the house with her new friends, friends whom I did not know. She never brought them home to meet us."

"If my mother loves me, she should come back to us and live with me and my father." These were Shirin's final words.

Didn't Shirin need her anymore? Could she live without her? Shirin was only thirteen, and she could choose whom she wanted to live with. She was a real person who had the right to choose! Mina was more than three times her age and she had not chosen what she had wanted until then. Now all of them, the court, Hamid and her own daughter wanted to deprive her of that.

• • •

While Shirin was in high school, Mina waited in front of her school on several occasions, watching her from afar. She left several phone messages for Shirin. When she did not receive a response, she called Hamid.

"Yes, she got your last message, but she erased it right away," Hamid sounded merciless. "It's not my fault; she doesn't want to talk to you."

In her senior year, Shirin was even taller than Hamid. Then she disappeared. Mina went to their house, her own old house, and waited in her car for hours. No sign of Shirin. One day Mina waited until Hamid came home and talked to him. His mostly gray hair had receded way above his forehead, and he looked more stooped.

"She went to New York last month," he said in the tone of a proud father. "She was accepted at NYU's journalism program."

"I can pay for her school. She doesn't need to know," Mina was in tears.

"She does not need your money. She has everything," he responded. "I have bought her a two bedroom apartment in Manhattan, close to her college." He got sarcastic. "You don't need to worry about her. She is doing great without you." Mina left angrily.

After a year, Mina called Hamid. He responded as cold as before. "No, she is not planning to come back to LA. She wants to stay there even after her school. I am thinking about selling my restaurants and moving to New York too." Mina cried and cried every time she hung up, but she kept calling gain.

"Ok, I will tell her you want to see her, but I am sure she will have the same response." Mina knew the response. "If my mom wants me, she should come and live with us."

It was only four months ago when Mina received Shirin's first email. A reply to the gifts and the letter Mina had sent for her twenty-first birthday.

Now, after eight years, she was going to see her daughter.

Mina's Revolution

New York - Sept. 11th 2001

<u>7:30 a.m.</u>

On her way out, Mina glanced at her image in the mirror for one last time. She pushed her bangs back. Now the sign of the old wound was so faded nobody noticed it except herself. She tucked a piece of hair behind her ear. She looked younger this way, but didn't like it. She drew her hair back and opened the buttons of her jacket. Still too formal. She took off the jacket and lay it on her forearm. She could fold it and put it on her briefcase during breakfast, and then put it on for the meeting. She shouldn't look too formal; it should just be a normal mother and daughter breakfast in a friendly atmosphere. Could it be that Shirin needed her for something now? No, Mina should not even ask her if she could be of any help. Was Shirin going to ask her to get back with Hamid? She put on the jacket, and in her way out, she picked up the newspaper left for her behind the door and tucked it in her briefcase.

The door attendant called a cab from the Taxis waiting line. "Madam is going to the World Trade Center." He opened the back door for Mina.

The driver made a U-turn and took the first right onto Fifth Avenue and another right into 57th Street. The traffic was much lighter than the usual Manhattan rush hours. Mina looked in the rearview mirror and pulled her hair behind her ears, and then looked at her watch. 4:20 am. It couldn't be that! She checked the watch again. Both the hour and minute-hand were stuck on four; the second-hand, motionless, stopped at six. She leaned forward and asked the time from the driver.

"It is ten past eight," answered the driver in a heavy Indian accent.

She was to meet Shirin at 8:30. "I want to be at WTC before 8:20. Do you think we can make it on time?"

"Yes ma'am. Don't worry, we will be there before that. It is just around the corner."

Good. She would have enough time to stop on the third floor, the corporate office, leave her briefcase and jacket, and then go to the restaurant. She could get back to the office after breakfast and respond to emails and messages before getting ready for the meeting.

The traffic became slower through the West Village. Mina looked at her watch again. Still four twenty. Why hadn't she fixed the time? She asked the driver again: "I am sorry, what time is it now?" The driver looked at her in the mirror and smiled, "Don't worry ma'am. We will be there soon." He sounded empathetic. Mina felt a sudden rush of tears in her eyes.

"Do you have children?" she asked gently.

"Oh, yes ma'am, plenty of them! Four boys and two daughters. All good students. Very smart. One in medical school, two in engineering."

The traffic was moving smoothly.

"Great! You are lucky," Mina was impressed. "How about the others?"

"My oldest daughter is married and the twin boys are still in elementary school," he looked at her in the mirror. "We had the twins after the older ones were almost on their own. My wife wanted to have more children at home."

Mina couldn't stop her curiosity, "It must be very expensive to raise so many kids in this city."

"Yes ma'am. It is very hard. Both my wife and I work all day to make ends meet."

When the driver turned onto Houston Street, the traffic suddenly came to a complete halt. Three cars had collided right in front of them. The driver made a hard sudden stop. Mina jolted but caught herself and sat back. The driver excused himself, got out of the car and went to check the situation. Mina waited for a few minutes. The driver was talking to a young women, apparently the driver of the other car. Mina peeked at the clock. 8:19 already. Mina rolled down the window and called to the driver. After a short delay, he returned to the car. "Fortunately I did not hit her. We can go. I am sorry for the delay." The traffic was jammed around them. It took him five more minutes to pull out from that lane and move to the left to turn onto Seventh Street. He did a U-turn on Liberty and stopped in front of the North Tower. It was 8:34. Mina gave him a twenty-dollar bill, opened the door, and got out.

She took her jacket off, then turned and checked herself in the passenger window for one last time. She could see a rough reflection of the World Trade Center's towers mixed with a distorted image of herself, as the cab began to move back into the traffic.

Mina turned and rushed to the building.

Mina's Revolution

About the Author

Mehrnoosh Mazarei was born and raised in Iran. She moved to Southern California in November 1979.

She co-founded and co-edited Forough, a Persian magazine dedicated to women's literature, between 1989 and 1991.

Ms. Mazarei has published four short story collections in Persian and a novel in English.

Her stories have been reviewed as outstanding Modernist stories in the text book "Short Story in Iran" and one of them was selected and anthologized as one of the ten best short stories published in 2004 in Iran.

Mazarei's stories have been published in the Narrative Magazine (USA), The Literary Review (USA), Eighty years Iranian Short Story (Iran), West Cost Line (Canada), Alef today (Syria) and Roadside Curiosities: Stories About American Pop Culture (Leipzig University).

She lives in Valley Center, California with her husband.